I0866569

Spector Books

... Oh! someone calling ... Hello? ...

Uh! I totally forgot the time

Hello dear reader,

I am a performer and choreographer, and 43 years old as I am writing this introduction. Welcome to this book! During spring 2022, still in the afterglow of the pandemic, I became increasingly curious about forms of documenting my work, as it is usually happening live and in the moment. Some time has already passed since I got involved with contemporary dance and performance around 1997, and although my life seems not yet over (currently I am kind of middle-aged, not dead yet etc. toi toi toi), I wanted to create an intuitive map, exploring how different places, times, conditions, and connections would mutually influence each other within 25 years of freelance work in the performative arts, both internationally and with a base in Eastern Germany.

Is there for example a link between the Peaceful Revolution of 1989/90 and my interest in chance operation and improvising? How would a participatory research format like *Resonanz – Postsocialist Group Improvisation*, developed with artist and writer Anna Zett in 2020-22 (see page 226) correspond with first self-made dances in empty flats or factories during the late 1990s? To what extent has the emergence of low-cost airlines in the 2000s influenced collaborative forms of work like *Pongo Land* (2008, with Nuno Lucas, page 156)? And what role does gentrification play, as an ongoing process I would encounter along the way in places like Berlin and Leipzig in the 1990s, 2000s, 2010s? How would this resonate in a self-organized space like the Fortuna Wetten (page 225) in the early 2020s?

While thinking about all this, I approached Igor Dobričić to join the process of making this publication. Igor is a dramaturge, we worked together for the first time in 2019 for *Singing Machine* (page 211). During our first conversations, Igor suggested to extend the idea of the book: what if, instead of focussing on my artistic work as a blueprint, really everything was taken into account? To make it literal in a radical sense, putting the story of a body next to traces of an artistic work, interweaving life and art-making.

Igor and I imagined this book to be a hybrid between a catalogue and a photo album based on a biography, which exists, like almost any biography, as a collection of images. Through this, establishing a chronology became more and more present, as we started our process with a selection of images ordered chronologically. Since I was a kid, I have had a fascination for historic traces, and although being quite bad at mathematics I love numbers and dates. So one evening in January 2023, I visited Igor with around 200 pictures in my pocket that we put on a table, following a timeline from 1981, the year of my birth, until 2022. For about three hours, we had a conversation, based on Igor asking questions along with the images. This talk quickly went beyond being an interview, as there were some motifs within both our lives that would enter in a specific constellation to each other, last but not least a post-communist condition of Igor being born in ex-Yugoslavia and me being born in the ex-GDR, and growing up in remaining bourgeois bubbles in Belgrade and Leipzig.

Luckily, Igor recorded this conversation, which became the base for a longer process of transcribing, compiling, putting text next to images, trying to make images dance. This took time, and new things happened that were completely unexpected. My mother fell ill and passed away in March 2023, which changed many aspects of my life, including this publication. I was making a book called *Timing* exactly in the moment I was losing a person who was very dear to me, and by nature connected to the process of my coming into life and growing up. So beyond "timing" in the sense of being a tool within being on stage, or "timing" in relation to certain decisions and moves I would take or make, there is a simple "timing" of life and its limitation that came to the fore here.

The following book belongs to a situation in between, at the cusp of something changing. Thanks to all dear people who supported the process! Susanne Ogan and Leonie Kusterer for gently structuring time (while I was stretching it), the fantastic team of Spector Books, in particular Christin Krause, Jan Wenzel and Natasha Agapova, who were tremendously helpful in making suggestions on form and ideas. Thanks to Bureau Ritter for making this publication possible in the frame of Tanzpakt Reconnect within the special circumstances of the Neustart Kultur Programme, and especially to my wife and long- time artistic companion Anne Zacho Søgaard, as well as Edith Zacho Heisig and Maja Zacho Heisig for spreading love, patience and some creative sparks. Also, the following pages would not exist without feedback and inspiration from dear colleagues, friends & family members Nuno Lucas, Thomas Proksch, Anna Zett, Jule Flierl, Diana Wesser, Marina Quesada, May Zarhy, Elpida Orfanidou, Nancy Böttner, Christiane Eisler, Johannes Heisig, Marcus Psurek, and Angelika Waniek.

Wishing you a joyful journey through the following pages!

HERMANN: Okay.
IGOR: So now you tell me.
HERMANN: Oh, good. From A to Z ...
IGOR: Just follow the pictures, and I will ask you questions.
HERMANN: Yeah. So I will try to say what is in the pictures or what these pictures represent to me. Let's start with this one, for example.
IGOR: This is before you were born, I think.
HERMANN: Yes. A weird picture; I am not sure if it's maybe from too long ago ...
IGOR: No, I think it is great—to connect something from long ago with a present moment of your life. That's the whole point of this.
HERMANN: It's a photo taken in the offices of Hermann Straube, my grand-grandfather from my mother's side, who was running a lottery business in Leipzig. With a big round lottery wheel in the foreground, in which all the tickets got mixed. And behind it, you see a picture of Stalin, the photo must have be taken somewhere in between 1945 and 1953.

My mother Christabel, before being a mother.
To her this publication is dedicated!

19

# 81

Physically, there is quite some similarity between my father and me, and looking at this picture of him standing on one leg, I was always curious. Because I do things like this on stage. → 13

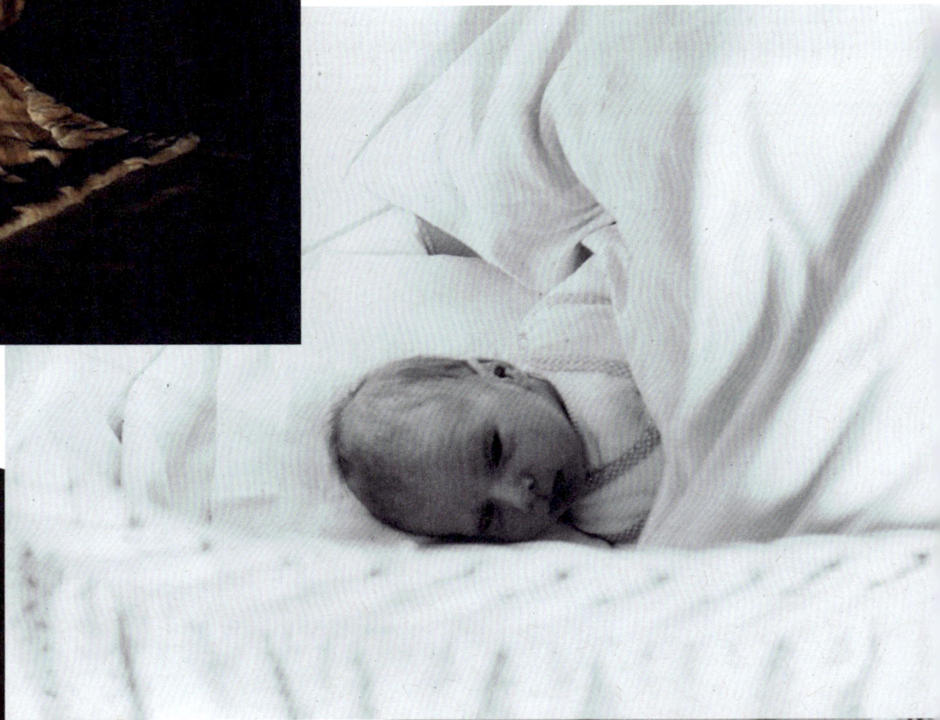

# 19

# 81

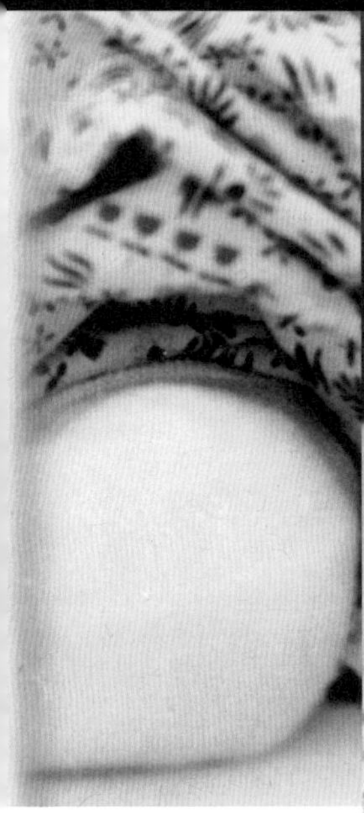

HERMANN: I mean, here in this picture from 1982—it's very, very early, and I'm certainly not "performing", but there is an aspect of play, of going against a limitation. Moreover, that moment where the baby flips onto its belly for the first time. Before, you have the baby lying on its back, still quite passive, not yet able to turn. Everything comes from above or is done to you. And then, suddenly, boom, there is this moment you flip onto your belly for the first time, looking at things from above. It's a huge thing.

IGOR: Oh, that's interesting. I never thought about this view.

HERMANN: And then you slowly expand your reach. You go here, you touch this ... gaining autonomy, gradually expanding your field of vision and your zone of action, of contacts. And that happens through play, and it's so difficult to distinguish. When does playing become performing? There is a consciousness developing and a kind of performing in front of your parents: If I do this, my parents will react like that ...

IGOR: Exactly. The beginning of performing. In psychological and phenomenological terms.

HERMANN: For example, this famous performance of "If I cry now, I might get an ice cream later."

IGOR: And it's interesting, the difference between the bodies—this body and that body.

HERMANN: Ah! You mean this picture of my father on one leg, in relation to my grandfather?

IGOR: Yeah. I mean, it's also a particular shift in self-perception—in the experience and understanding of the artist's body. Your father, there, standing on one leg; it's almost conceptual art.

HERMANN: For sure there's also something about different generations. I mean, if you look at the body of my father's father, I see it for sure influenced by the war and the ideology working through him. He was born in 1925, part of a generation formed by the Nazi regime, the war, and after that, many years of communism. So inside the conception of what a man should be, there was not much space for emotionality. And an issue with touch, for example. And my father—I see him being marked much more by post-1968 pop culture, even within a GDR context. So it's another body. Physically, there is quite some similarity between my father and me, and looking at this picture with him standing on one leg, I was always curious because I do things like this on stage. The picture was taken on the balcony of the flat where I used to spend my childhood, Lassallestrasse 6 in 7010 Leipzig, GDR.

→ 9

IGOR: It's a very interesting photo because it's already coming close to your own performative practice, in a way. For whatever reason, even then, there was a certain shift from the material object towards a live event. There is this modernist tradition of art-making, coming from a certain long lineage of male crafting, which then got questioned in the 1960s and 70s, creating as well a stage for your father to perform on the balcony. Which is no longer reducible to the act of crafting. It's rather an immediate, embodied creative gesture. And there is something about this history that speaks not only about a shift in art from object to live event, but also about the way gender politics affect it. And it's kind of relevant because, despite the impression that there is a break away from the family lineage in your art-making, you actually followed this lineage in its transformation during the 1960s and 1970s, departing even further from the modernist paradigm of the masculine and muscular artist as craftsman that existed in the past.

gradually expanding
the zone of activity

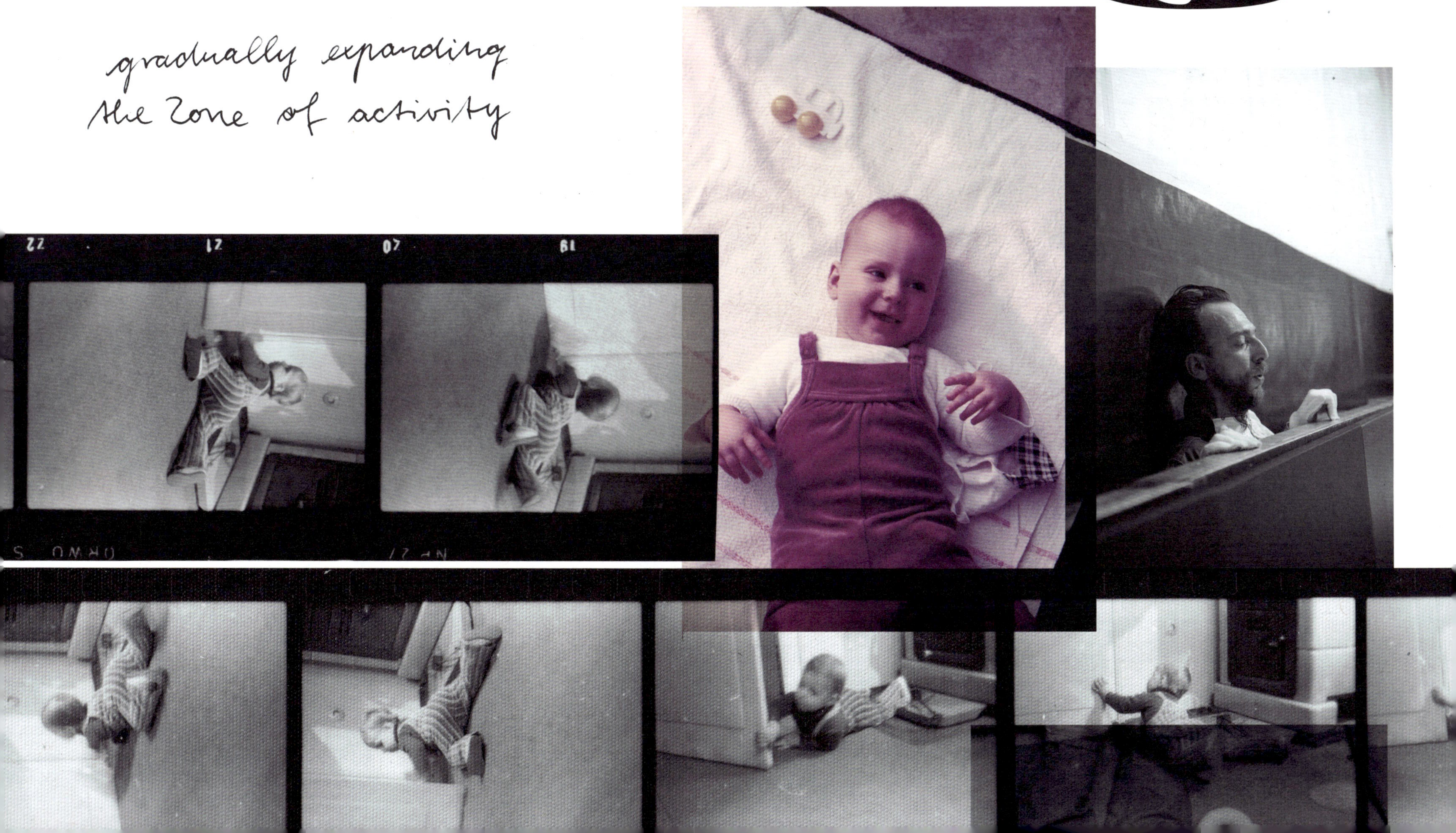

playing as a base
for performing?

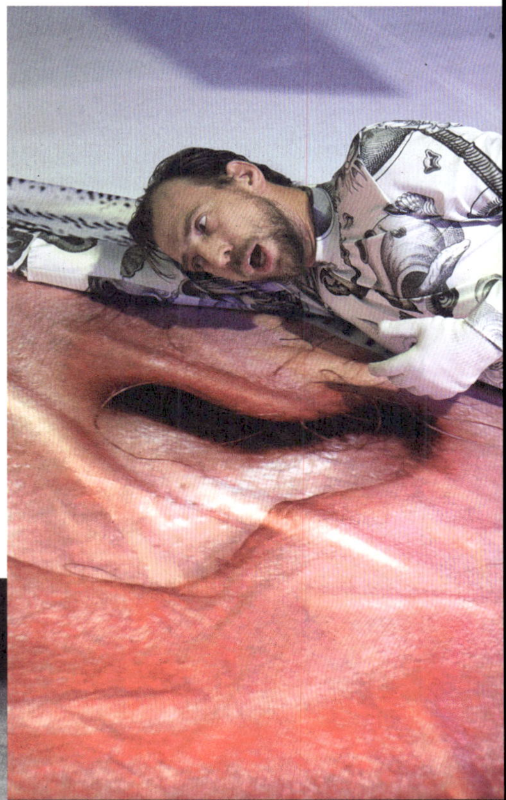

82

A projection → 18

02

meeting "Großmama"
Brunhild Eisler

→ 16

HERMANN: Here you see my father Johannes and my uncle Walter Eisler as young painters, wanting to surprise my grandfather Bernhard on his birthday by re-staging a picture taken in 1924 of his father, Walter Heisig, who was a painter as well, in Breslau/ Wrocław. In 1983, my aunt Christiane Eisler took these shots of both brothers posing, wearing a white suit, and holding a white brush. I was around, and instinctively they put me in a white suit and gave me the brush. A projection.

IGOR: That's super fascinating. Transmission through the generations.

HERMANN: The funny thing is that it was not so surprising in the end, as they found out that my grandfather had done the same thing back in the 1950s: re-staging the picture of his father with a white suit and a white brush. But like that, this series of pictures came into being, painting in different conditions and places throughout the 1920s, the 1950s, the 1980s.

IGOR: There is another thing I want to address. Until now, we were talking a lot about "fathers". I mean, there is something about transmission from father to son. It is very strong because there are these three generations of artists. So somehow, for what you do, this is certainly relevant. But what is missing from that picture are "mothers". There is something about "mothers" which is also relevant to keep in mind ...

HERMANN: That's really true. For example, I am thinking a lot about my paternal grandmother, Brunhild Heisig Eisler, my grandfather's first wife. Last year in Fortuna, my love Anne Zacho Søgaard was guiding a session where participants would meditate about mothers in their families. You would choose someone to concentrate on; I chose my father's mother, and I realized again how much I am affected by my paternal grandmother. She was a very creative person, full of life. After the divorce with my grandfather, she was a single mother in the 1950s and 1960s, raising my uncle and my father. Among other things, she worked as a book illustrator and costume designer,

and as a freelancer, she occasionally designed exhibition stands for the Leipzig Trade Fair. There she got to know a man from Frankfurt am Main, and they fell in love, towards the end of the 1950s. For about half a year, my grandmother sent my father and my uncle to live with her parents, while she partly moved to West Germany, to Frankfurt. She had plans to take her sons with her, and there was a vague idea to go to Canada later. But then my grandfather didn't want to let the kids go, which forced my grandmother to come back to Leipzig. Soon after that, in 1961, the Wall was built, also ending the relationship with the man my grandmother was in love with.

IGOR: How old were you when she died?

HERMANN: I was 25, so we had the chance to get to know each other and spend time together. In the middle of the eighties, she lived at our place for some months, and often picked me up from kindergarten. After a stroke in 1988, she could only speak and walk very slowly, and towards the end of her life, she was affected by multiple illnesses. So gender inequality and male-female relations really do play a role here, and it is necessary to retrospectively speak about that, to say, okay, despite his fame, let's not give my grandfather all the credit, and instead put him in a bigger context, inside another fabric, another time perspective.

IGOR: Mothers and fathers.

HERMANN: Mothers and fathers.

A cosmos of its own, a kind of bubble that inspired my imagination a lot as a child. → 22

79

# 83

hanging out in the garden
protected against the outside world

HERMANN: These are my grandparents from the mother's side.

IGOR: What is their story?

HERMANN: Oh! Difficult to say in short. Ultimately, I would say they were conserving a concept of bourgeois life in the middle of communism, which resulted in a quite different treatment of space, of social relations—performing bourgeois space outside of its proper context.

IGOR: I know that from my father's family in Yugoslavia. Trying to resist communism inside of a private domain. Because in public, you could not perform the bourgeois family properly anymore, but in private, everything is still maintained.

→ 21

HERMANN: Yes, that was also the way my maternal grandparents handled life. Their house in Leipzig was a cosmos of its own, a kind of bubble that inspired my imagination a lot as a child. I spent much time there, as my mother was close to my grandparents, and they would take care of me when my mother was not around. They were running a lottery business that my grandfather's father had established.

IGOR: Really? Lottery?

HERMANN: Yes, it was named after my grandfather's father, Hermann Straube, who founded it in 1899. My great-grandfather was born in 1870 in a village south of Leipzig. Around 1890, he was moving to the city, where he became wealthy from running the lottery in the 1920s.

IGOR: So he took his chances.

HERMANN: Yes, dealing with the customers' desire for chance, my grandfather's father was able to transform the social situation for himself and his family. But then other things happened, the war came and this idea of steady progress was broken, but lived on as a ghost.

IGOR: The same chance that you took, took care of you.

HERMANN: My mother's father—I think he always felt a bit in debt to his father, who had built up the business. In the 1950s, he planned to move to West Germany, but would not leave Leipzig as long as his father was still alive. And when my great-grandfather finally died in early 1961, my grandparents prepared everything to leave the GDR. But then the Berlin Wall was built in August 1961, and they were locked in.

IGOR: Because chance has two sides.

HERMANN: So my mother's father remained a businessman, even under communist conditions, falling out of time, trying to keep things together. Maybe that was his life's mission. In 1975, the state nationalized the lottery, and my grandfather turned 65. So when I was a child, I would learn to know my grandparents as lucky pensioners who were able to travel to the West.

Did you see this picture? For me, it's a lot about the bourgeois body, as it's also about performing a certain kind of seriousness.

IGOR: Trained, not only artistically, but also socially.

HERMANN: Yes. With my mother's mother, for example, I had a very warm, physical relationship. But I also sensed the difference, for example, when there was a bigger social situation. My grandmother would then start to play a different "role" than when we were together in private.

IGOR: You are talking about gender roles in the bourgeois family. But now you are involved in running Fortuna, so in a way, you are fulfilling your family destiny.

HERMANN: Not sure. I imagine the Hermann Straube Lottery as a calculated system, a relationship between a number of winning and losing lottery tickets. I feel the way I deal with chance is quite the opposite of this. I don't design a system.

IGOR: No, but you do gamble.

HERMANN: That's true.

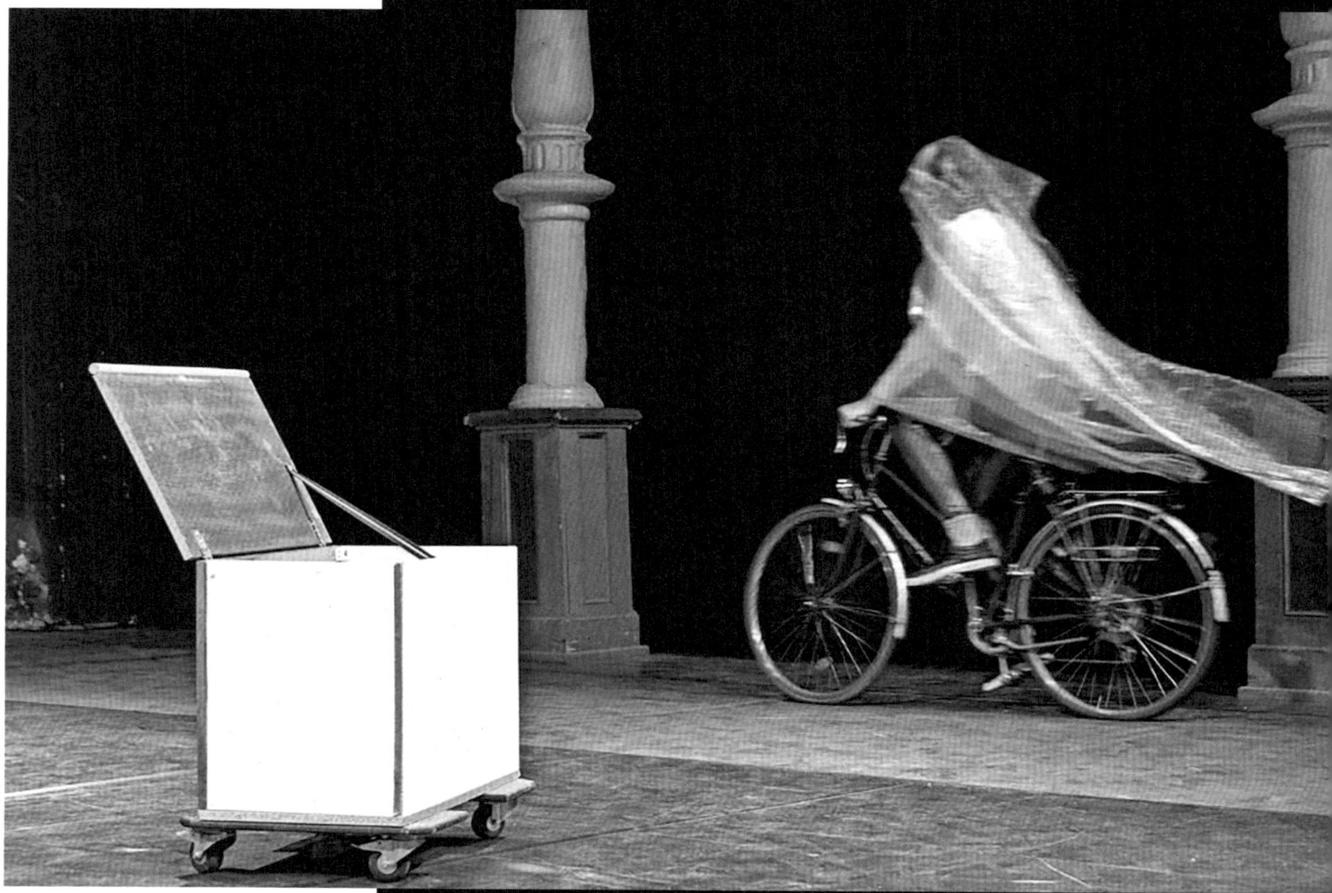

# 84

an only child

→ 33

HERMANN: This picture over here was probably taken at the beginning of the 1980s. My father's father, as head of the art school in Leipzig, in front of a painting of his. It's interesting, his body here, how he performs this masculine attitude, accustomed to explaining things, maybe even feeling comfort in being able to quickly and sharply respond, as a public figure.

IGOR: But what was your relationship with your grandfather when you were a child? Did you relate to him? And when did he die?

HERMANN: In 2011. There was a relationship for many years but it was not so intimate. I mean, my grandfather was not really within reach because he would work most of the time. I would visit him together with my father, and as he could feel a certain discomfort sitting in family situations, he would often receive us in his studio. When I was 13, he would come to me and say: Junge, boy, you need a Schnaps. And then I would be polite and drink it sip by sip. Some kind of initiation. As a child, I would call him "Opa Bernhard", but I think he was not happy with that role. As I grew up, it became a little easier for us to connect.

IGOR: Did you recognize the status of your grandfather and your father at that time as a form of fame? You were aware of it in these terms?

HERMANN: I think so, yes. Once I started reading, I was curious to discover catalogs, articles, trying to understand what was happening. And also, on different occasions, during exhibition openings or birthdays, as a single child, I was immersed in different kinds of conversations of the adults, and I think I was good at copying them in having small talk. At the same time, with all these family members associated with painting, I also often experienced this kind of question following the projection. "What about you? Are you maybe interested in painting as well?"

IGOR: But you escaped it. That's what you did at the end of the day. Maybe your whole artistic trajectory is an escape route?

HERMANN: I don't see it so much as an escape, at least not from the artworks of my father, uncle, or grandfather that continue to resonate with me. In the end, I was drawn simply somewhere else, wanting to experience other types of relations to the body, to material, to time. And if I would have studied painting, let's say in the art school in Leipzig, I would imagine it still indirectly being linked to my father, my grandfather, and the debate of abstraction versus figurative painting. Everything would feel, in a way, like a statement, or at least in relation to—

IGOR: Everything is kind of codified.

HERMANN: And I think, in a very different way, that was what my grandfather was busy with, navigating strict political conventions and codes, finding a specific artistic language in relation to these frictions, throughout different periods of ideological pressure and liberalization within GDR cultural politics, ultimately examining the constraints of socialist realism in order to find a way to deal with his trauma of the Second World War. In 1942, as a 17-year-old, he joined the 12th SS Panzer Division "Hitlerjugend" as a volunteer, surviving the offensive in the Ardennes as well as the battles in his hometown of Breslau, which was declared a "fortress" at the beginning of 1945. In 2006, I joined my grandfather on a trip to Wrocław, and although I felt he initially rejected any emotionality towards revisiting the city, it was important for us to be there together.

→ 144

19

# 85

This picture over here was probably taken at the beginning of the 1980s. My father's father, as head of the art school in Leipzig, in front of a painting of his. It's interesting, his body here, how he performs this masculine attitude, accustomed to explaining things, maybe even feeling comfort in being able to quickly and sharply respond, as a public figure. → 30

# 05

# 19

looking at a Concorde
landing like an UFO at Leipzig/Halle airport
during Trade fair times

# 86

HERMANN: Talking about the muscular and craft-related paradigm, there is this drumming picture here. I was seven years old, I think. There is a situation attached to it happening in my father's studio in the art school in Dresden. This must have been around 1988, the time when my parents were in the process of separation.

IGOR: What were the drums doing in the artist's studio?

HERMANN: I think the drum kit became part of several paintings, but at the same time I guess my father himself was drumming a little bit, from time to time. So the drum kit was there, and I started to play with it. The story goes that I got very frustrated, crying because I was unable to drum in the way I imagined it.

→ 42

IGOR: Do you have a memory of it, or is it a family story?

HERMANN: I still remember the sense of frustration. It occurred several times in my life later on: me imagining doing something and then, while trying it, getting into conflict with myself about what I am not able to do, what I am failing to master.

IGOR: Talking about the tradition, craft, and the place of mastery in it all.

HERMANN: Yes. To me, it is also related to what happened later: me throwing myself into dance without any training. So there is something in there that relates to the same subject.

IGOR: Coming back to this question of performing: for me it really is a practical question. Where does it start, and what does it entail?

HERMANN: Um. I mean, looking at some of the pictures from the 1980s, there is of course a connection to children's games. For example, as a six- or seven-year-old child, I would like to dress up, playing with different roles—a cook, a king, an actress, a waiter. I was fascinated with the different ways people would dress and how they would "perform" their role. Like in this picture from 1993, mimicking a singer on TV, also a kind of "rehearsal".

IGOR: In a conventional biography, you know, there would be a discourse on how you always liked to perform ... So of course, the question is, isn't it that every kid likes to perform? Isn't this universal?

HERMANN: To a certain degree, of course it is. I also witness that a lot with my own children. At this age of five, six, or seven, through personal experience or the media, you are confronted with different roles that adults play. And as a way of processing, there is a joy in mimicking, repeating, making things your own.

IGOR: That's what kids do.

HERMANN: And for me, that is very close to the joy of performing. It's testing your relationship to the others.

IGOR: Let's put it this way, there is a strong component of mimicking the life of grown-ups in the development of a child. I still wonder what's the real meaning of that because we take it for granted. We kind of laugh at it, and we kind of find it amusing. But I always wonder what is actually happening there. Is there something there that is relevant for understanding what we as people engaged in performing arts are doing? What are the kids performing, you know, and for whom and why? There is a certain journey of something being carried through to a point where it becomes public.

→ 75

19

around adults

86

The drum kit was there, and I started to play with it. The story goes that I got very frustrated, crying because I was unable to drum in the way I imagined it. → 38

# 87

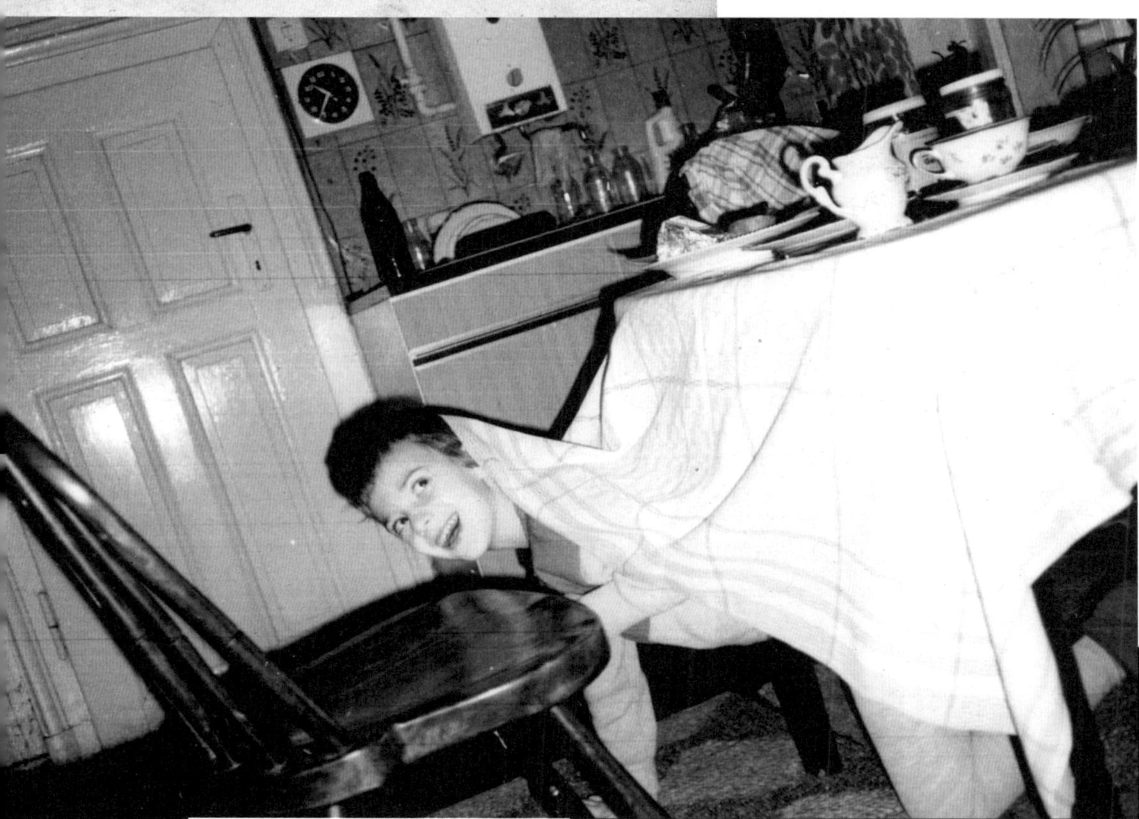

Palast der Republik

82

at an official 1st of May demonstration

# 10

Members of the socialist youth organization, the Young Pioneers. We were visiting our "Patenbrigade", a collective at the publisher Verlag für die Frau in Leipzig, during a Christmas celebration. → 48

→ 52

IGOR: And who is this with you on the sofa?
HERMANN: This is my friend, Sarah. We met in 1988, and we are still friends today.
IGOR: Do you still have friends from your childhood?
HERMANN: Yes. For example, Sarah and I got to know each other when we started school in 1988, and our mothers became friends as well. Later, we lost touch a bit but re-met as teenagers, exploring the nightlife of the nineties. Later, in 2002, we became roommates in Berlin.
IGOR: And what is Sarah doing now?
HERMANN: She is a scriptwriter and film director. Among other projects, she made a great movie called *Transpapa*. About her father changing gender—leaving the GDR to the West and becoming a woman.
IGOR: Really?
HERMANN: It's a very special story, changing the political system, which leads to changing gender.
IGOR: And what are the costumes that you are wearing in this picture?
HERMANN: This was around in 1989 in our apartment, enacting fairy tales and movies ... And this picture here shows the two of us again, in 1988, wearing something else as members of the socialist youth organization, the Young Pioneers. We were visiting our "Patenbrigade", a collective at the publisher Verlag für die Frau in Leipzig, during a Christmas celebration ... Actually, I feel it was very clever how the communist dictatorship was introducing performative elements ... and they really got me, I think, when I was seven. Wearing these uniforms, and on top of that, having a kind of document confirming our membership in the organization. So when we would vote or support a decision, we would raise our hand, holding our membership card up in the air, like at a party meeting. I remember enjoying this, feeling like a respected part of socialist society for a moment.

→ 47

IGOR: We had the same in Yugoslavia ... Pioneers.
HERMANN: Yes.

IGOR: And we had an initiation date and photos of ourselves with a blue hat. And, uh, this white shirt that always had to be ironed. I still have it, actually, in one of the boxes. A small photo on a small piece of fabric, like silk, which said, "On this day when I become a pioneer, I solemnly swear ... " That was the way it worked for me. Which probably was not so different for you.

HERMANN: No, it was not. It's interesting that you would swear—in the GDR, I remember something like the ten commandments, similar to the Bible: We young pioneers honor our parents ... But also things like: We young pioneers always keep our bodies healthy and clean. A quite uncanny, totalitarian aspect of body control.

IGOR: Healthy and clean—

HERMANN: But what was also strange was that, in my case, I entered this system for only one year, until it disappeared all of a sudden. My first day of school was in September 1988. And already one year later, when the next school year was about to begin, things began to disintegrate. I remember being invited to a children's birthday, and I still remember the host's name, Alexa, partly because just one week later, she was gone, probably with her parents through the open border between Hungary and Austria. None of the teachers would talk about it. And then everything went so quickly. A few weeks later, I attended some of the big Monday demonstrations in Leipzig when it was safe to go, around November 1989. While walking down the streets with my friend Sarah, our mothers, and 470 000 other people, chanting slogans like "Sta-si- in-die Pro-duk-tion!" (Let the Stasi do manual labor!), I still remember the specific shape of Sarah's umbrella.

19

8

8

# 19

This is my friend, Sarah. We met in 1988. → 48

89

# 19

It's strange, I have difficulties finding pictures for the radical change that took place in 1989/90 and the enormous transformations that followed. → 58

89

Growing up in the 1980s, we encountered these institutions, the bourgeois family and the church, in a moment of crisis. Marginalised during communism, but still existing in niches. → 228

# 1990

→ 54

HERMANN: It's strange, I have difficulties finding pictures for the radical change that took place in 1989/90 and the enormous transformations that followed. And later, looking at these pictures of the early nineties, with capitalism knocking at the door. Recently, there has been a larger discourse and much more discussion about the chaos and violence of the early 1990s in Eastern Germany, and I became more consciously aware of the context I was growing up in: I lived in a larger city, in a liberal bubble, I was economically stable, I was male, all this ... Maybe I project too much into it, but I think after 1990, all this resulted in some kind of feeling of: Now the whole world is open to me.
IGOR: As communism is gone—
HERMANN: Yes, and as in 1990, the West German structures were hastily applied to East Germany, all of a sudden, the former GDR would be a part of "the West", of NATO, of the European Union. And having the new passport of the Federal Republic meant new possibilities for studying abroad, for example. Throughout the nineties, being young and flexible, to me, things sometimes felt like, "Now you have to make something nice of it!" Having my grandparents' and parents' generation in mind, struggling with all these cracks of the East German twentieth century. So there was an underlying feeling that I should do something with this lucky timing.
IGOR: Use your luck—do you really remember that you felt like that then? I think it's now hindsight.
HERMANN: Half and half, I guess. But I remember feeling an air of what Francis Fukuyama called "The End of History" at the time. This mindset located somewhere between October 1989 and September 2001 ... At least in the greater part of Europe, the borders were opening. And as I eagerly watched the news and read the newspapers, on my knees, on the floor of the living room in the early nineties, I imagined finally some wounds of the past could heal. Within the cityscape of Leipzig, a lot of renovation took place, which made a big change after

hearing the adults in the eighties talk about depression and decay. Many people I knew would live in houses constructed around 1900, and in all the decor, there were always traces of a lost prosperity. And I fantasized about a return to splendor, mixing it with a somewhat more Americanized imagination of skyscrapers, neon design, fashion magazines, etc.

IGOR: And it's so funny because this is precisely the time that I went through hell. So it's a bizarre opposition of perspectives because when all this started for you in the nineties, for me, it was the most terrible decade of my life. Which actually is exactly the opposite because in communist Yugoslavia we had a passport that allowed absolute freedom of travel. So my communism was not your communism. We were not rich in any sense, but in the eighties, I could travel abroad regularly. And all of that disappeared in 1989, the same year. So there is an inversion. A mirror image—and all of a sudden, my passport was worth nothing.

HERMANN: That's crazy.

IGOR: It's completely crazy when you think about it. So I was coming from this kind of—how to say—anti-story of yours. In the very same decade.

HERMANN: Yes.

IGOR: For me, the end of history is something entirely different. I mean, I'm just kind of fascinated with realizing this in this conversation. Because the end of history across the divide between different ideologies looks very different.

HERMANN: Mhm.

IGOR: What is white to you is black to me.

# 1990

Test the West

divieto di
fermata
VIA SACRA

Catholicism is super theatrical. → 109

# 91

HERMANN: In 1991, when I was nine years old, after the changes of 1989/90, my mother took the initiative to have me baptized.

IGOR: So it's coming from your mother's side.

HERMANN: Yes, ultimately through her mother's father. He was born around 1890 close to the Danish border, a very Protestant area, then relocated to the south of Germany and became Catholic, which is why my grandmother, and through this, her children, my uncle and my mother, became Catholic as well.

IGOR: Converts make the most passionate Catholics.

HERMANN: Yes! And he was very interested in theater. His daughter, my grandmother, would rarely go to church in the 1950s and 1960s. But then, in the 1970s, my mother's brother Christof Straube became a member of an association of students under the umbrella of the Catholic Church. This association was attractive to many young people critical to the communist state, and this is where he revived religiosity again for himself and my mother.

IGOR: So it came from an alternative place—

HERMANN: Yes. Because in the context of the GDR, this Catholic student association would offer another type of freedom, which was very attractive.

IGOR: Were there many Catholics in the GDR?

HERMANN: It was a small minority. I would say about 4% of the population.

IGOR: But was it tolerated?

HERMANN: There were different phases in the history of the GDR. In the 1950s, it was sanctioned more harshly. Later, Catholicism was kind of tolerated, as long as the church didn't touch the political order. And also, within its forty years of existence, the GDR was very successful in turning people into atheists.

IGOR: But your mother was religious?

HERMANN: Yes. In the seventies, within this Catholic student organization, it was also a matter of weaving a fabric of community independent of the state. I think in that sense, spirituality arrived in connection with friendship and a shared criticism of the communist system. Which I think was not anticommunist in a conservative sense either. For example, they discussed liberation theology from South America. There was a search for a "third way" between communism and capitalism, inspired by early Christianity.

IGOR: It's so funny. Because in my family, it's the other way around. The religiosity comes from my father's side, also from a more bourgeois mentality. With my mother, it's different. Her father, my grandfather, whom I never knew because he died before I was born, was a very famous Yugoslav partisan in the Second World War. And so my mother's family was not interested in religion at all. Back in Yugoslavia, religion was not encouraged but never sanctioned. Did you read Saint Augustine?

HERMANN: No, never.

IGOR: You should read his *Confessions*! His story is quintessential, especially for the Catholic Church. But in a way, it's not only about the church. It's also about spirituality. And it's about the form which actually relates to what we are doing here—a narration of one's own life.

HERMANN: Ah—crazy.

IGOR: *Confessions* is a complete, thorough analysis of himself—from the moment he was born all the way to the moment when he's narrating. Like us, he is starting from a year zero. And then he goes through years one, two, three, four, etc. But before that, he also goes backward and asks a question about what happened while he was still in his mother's womb. So it started before he was born. In a certain sense, we are also asking that question when we, for example, look at this picture of your grandparent's lottery business—

Turning 10 years old

# 1991

postsocialist carnival (Klasse 4b)

92

# 1992

different generations
climbing the same type of tree
1992/2021

HERMANN: In 1992, when I was ten years old, I started at the Evangelisches Schulzentrum Leipzig, a school newly founded after the changes of 1989/90 under the umbrella of the Protestant church. To me, that was an important place. The teachers were a mix of Christian East German teachers critical of the communist school system and some young, rather progressive teachers who had come from West Germany. A place that was less influenced by GDR pedagogy.

IGOR: But what was there that was absent from a communist school?

HERMANN: I think there was a difference, for example, in physical education. Do you remember those communist PE teachers?

IGOR: Yeah, I know. Next to the bourgeois body discipline, you have a communist body discipline as well. Physical excellence once more.

HERMANN: Luckily, I was never sporty enough to be selected into the GDR competitive sports system, but even in conventional sports education, there were lots of authoritarian traces, and I profoundly hated this. And of course, apart from sports, there were authoritarian elements in pedagogy, mainly within the way of teaching, the role of the teacher ... And I was thankful for structures breaking away from this in order to gain space for a certain autonomy in thinking and doing.

IGOR: It connects to what you said about the nineties. You wanted to go forward, to look ahead. And, to a certain degree, your own aesthetics are shaped by that, aren't they?

HERMANN: Maybe it's a search for a different world on the stage, some kind of temporary utopia, undermining or countering reality. I like it when things become strange or dreamy. So, one part of my artistic interest is definitely leaning towards creating imaginary landscapes, which includes a fascination for futuristic aesthetics. The sound of an eighties' synthesizer—

IGOR: But there is a paradox. I think that the futurism

that you have a fascination for is a kind of amalgam between the past and the future.

HERMANN: Sure! Because the future already has a past. But it's true, traces of the past do always keep me busy. For example, this picture from 1995. It was taken on a hiking trip to the Czech Republic with my father. In the woods, we found the ruins of a chapel, and I was digging out parts of gravestones lying around to see what was written there. Being eleven, twelve, thirteen years old, I had this wish to become an archeologist. I imagined digging out or restoring things and discovering what was written there and by whom. There is a curiosity about traces—how a building, a landscape, or even a gesture would change through the flow of time, including misunderstandings, cracks, U-turns, expansions. You can never completely foresee these processes. I think it's also why I was never drastically moving to another place, leaving Germany or Europe, for example.

IGOR: I mean, it was not necessary, if one thinks of the dramatic events that were taking place in Germany itself, in a way.

HERMANN: Yes. I was always sufficiently—

IGOR: Both challenged and stimulated by what is going on.

HERMANN: And I had this urge to keep a relationship with the place I come from. It was always very strong.

IGOR: Yeah.

HERMANN: That's why moving to Berlin after 2000 was perfect because I could remain close to Leipzig, but at the same time, a whole different world would open for me.

IGOR: So the link to the past was always implicitly kind of—present.

HERMANN: I never did a total cut.

IGOR: I think this is also related to what you said just before, that you wanted to be an archaeologist. So there is some essential bond with the past, which is also characterized in you.

HERMANN: Yes.

993

# 1993

a Period I was obsessed with history & nobility,
even to the point of researching some
obscure abdicated dynasties,
copying their postures

# 19

This book found me, the autobiography of Ruth Klüger, a survivor of the Holocaust. A german youngster reading about Auschwitz in the holidays

→ 84

HERMANN: I was living with my mom, we had a somewhat symbiotic relationship. Most of my childhood, until the mid-nineties, we lived in this quite large apartment, originally through the GDR Artists' Association, paying 260 marks for 145 square meters.
IGOR: The two of you? That's enormous. What were you doing in 145 m²?
HERMANN: Well, we didn't use all the spaces in order not to have to heat everything. Also, during the afternoons or when my mother went out in the evenings occasionally, I stayed at home alone. In the nineties, people got more afraid of crime, and there was this wave of crime stories in the newspaper and on TV. I developed a whole fantasy when hearing noises alone at night. I had a plan A and a plan B for what to do if somebody broke in. But otherwise, my mom and I, we spent a lot of time in our living room, which we called "Octagon" as it had eight corners and light from above, but no windows, which added to a feeling of being slightly cut off from everyday life, in a good way. In the end, I think I might have spent much more time there than in my room.
IGOR: It's interesting how the images that are relating to your mother are images about interiors and enclosed, private spaces—the home. And the images related to your father are more about exteriors—being in nature or in public spaces.
HERMANN: I think that's quite true! Growing up with my mother, there was a lot of exchange through eating together, watching the news, listening to music; books would play an important role. We were sharing a joy in observing and reflecting on what would happen around us, and my mother had a fantastic sense of humor. From the end of the 1970s until around 1995, my mother was working at a publishing house, Edition Leipzig. She would work as an editor, proofreading art books and museum guides. After the changes of 1989/90, Edition Leipzig was shrinking, from sixty employees to about four, and my mother

had to change her profession, working for an advertising agency until 2022.

IGOR: Your mother's family is about domesticity: Contained internal spaces coupled with a notion of family and intimate relation to home. And then your father's family, three generations of artists married to the arts, always kind of breaking out of the frame, out of that domestic context—moving out, reinventing themselves, yet still depending on it, in a way.

HERMANN: There's also a very different connection to objects. My mother developed a long-lasting bond with her green sofa, for example. She had it for more than forty-five years—the same sofa.

IGOR: Really?

HERMANN: From the end of the 1970s throughout the eighties, the nineties, and the zeros—in that sense, my mom didn't follow the trend to change furniture in the nineties, after the fall of communism. In 1996, my mom and I had to move out of the apartment I spent my childhood in, and I absolutely refused to help. The house we were living in got restituted to the heirs of the pre-war owners, who sold it to an investor, and then we all had to move out and go to another place. That's a story that later, during the years after 2000, I was to repeat three times over in Berlin—a kind of post-socialist running gag. Having to move out because the house was sold to investors and would get redeveloped—

→ 92

IGOR: The beginning of gentrification. I find it fascinating. This sudden shift from a socialist ideological privilege toward the market brutality of neoliberal capitalism. And also this historical revisionism where the old bourgeoisie got restitution only to quickly sell on what they got back—

# 19

an attempt to cut back some plants → 88

# 94

a somewhat symbiotic relationship. → 80

19

# 95

This is a New Year's Eve party in 1995/6, and together with my father, I would perform this sketch, *Dinner for One*. → 88

HERMANN: Jumping ahead to 1994 … At that time, every second or third weekend I would take a train and visit my father in Dresden, where he was living together with Antoinette, a very inspiring artist and painter. This photo was taken in their garden during an attempt to cut back some plants. When my father became head of the art school in Dresden in 1988, the city offered him to buy a house for thirty thousand East German marks, by chance located on a street called Malerstrasse—what an address! After 1990, it turned out that the grounds this house was built upon had been Jewish property taken away by the Nazis and given to another family, probably one close to the Nazi apparatus. They built the house but left during the communist times. And then these two parties, the two previous owners, came back after the fall of the Berlin Wall, both claiming the house. My father had to move out in the year 2000, and I don't know exactly what happened in the end, it was a complicated legal case. But in 1994, my father and Antoinette were still living there. It was an influential time for me, and I would learn a lot from them. After stepping back from his position at the art school, my father would jump into working as a freelancer within the conditions of the capitalist art market, a whole different chapter opening up for him. At this time, we would start to connect differently, through conversations, taking trips together, and last but not least through humor. For sure, this was influenced by the fact that when I visited my father, this would always happen in my spare time. Both my father and Antoinette have a talent for friendship and hosting people. For example, going back to this picture: This is a New Year's Eve party in 1995/6, and together with my father, I would perform this sketch, *Dinner for One*, maybe also as a pedagogical exercise to improve my English. *Dinner for One* is very popular in Germany. Each year, it gets repeated on TV, and the basic principle of this sketch is also repetition. Like many

→ 83

→ 86

others, I watched it many times. It's only about 15 minutes long, about a woman who celebrates her ninetieth birthday, and she invites four friends. But the problem is that none of these friends are alive anymore. So the butler, apart from serving five different courses, has to impersonate all the characters and cheer and drink for each absent guest. By doing this, he is gradually getting more and more out of control. The butler is played by a great actor, Freddie Frinton. He has a fantastic physicality, which was super inspiring to me.

IGOR: That's important. I mean, in a strange way—because there is a particular physicality to it.

HERMANN: Funnily enough, it also refers to the bourgeois world, it's about a gradual loss of control while keeping certain rules and protocols. And as we acted it out at this New Year's Eve party in 1995, people reacted quite enthusiastically.

IGOR: And your father, was he playing the female role?

HERMANN: Yes, he had shaved his beard to play Miss Sophie.

IGOR: And how old were you?

HERMANN: I had just turned 14. So I think around this time I began to feel an instinctive drive toward the situation of a performance. More than in other artistic practices, I would feel at ease dealing with the specific energies of that situation. And some people around me felt that as well.

checking out the living room
dressed up as Miss Marple

# 1996

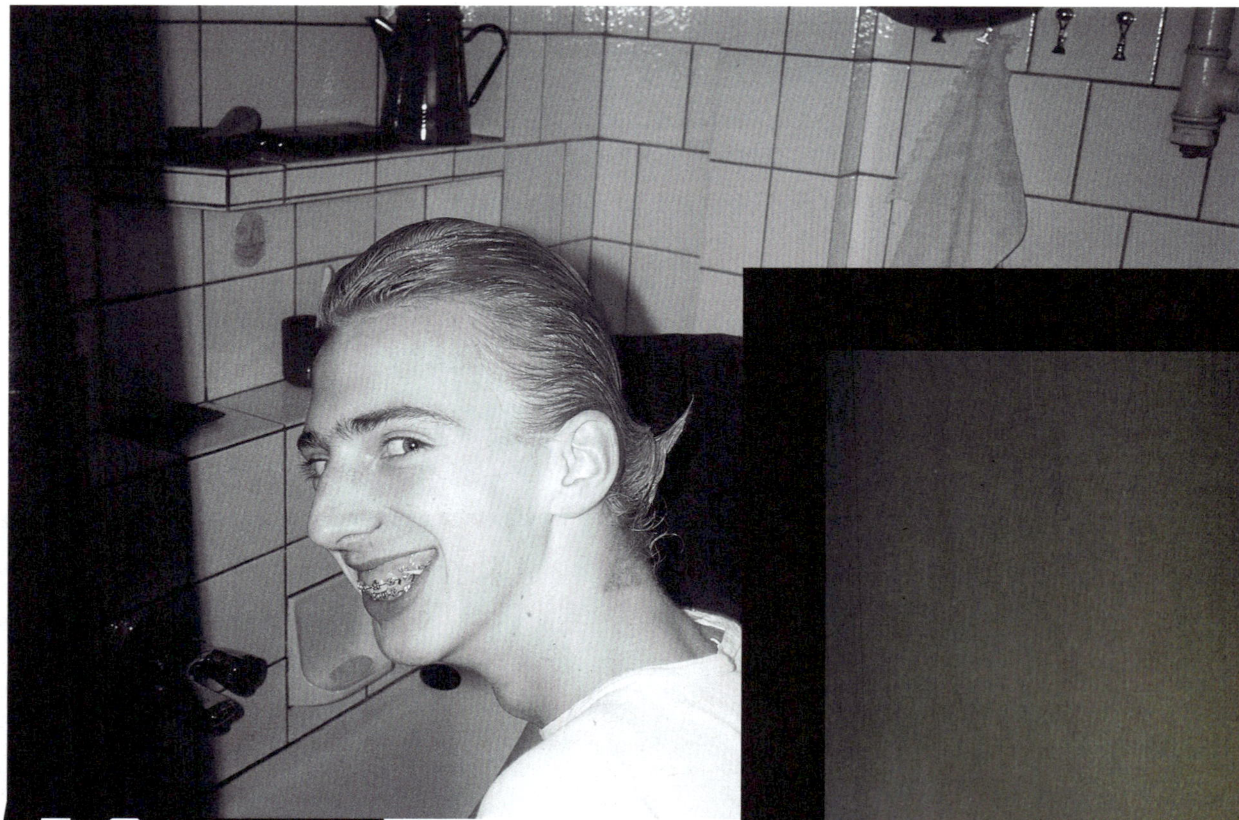

# 1996

In 1996, my mom and I had to move out of the apartment I spent my childhood in, and I absolutely refused to help. → 81

# 19

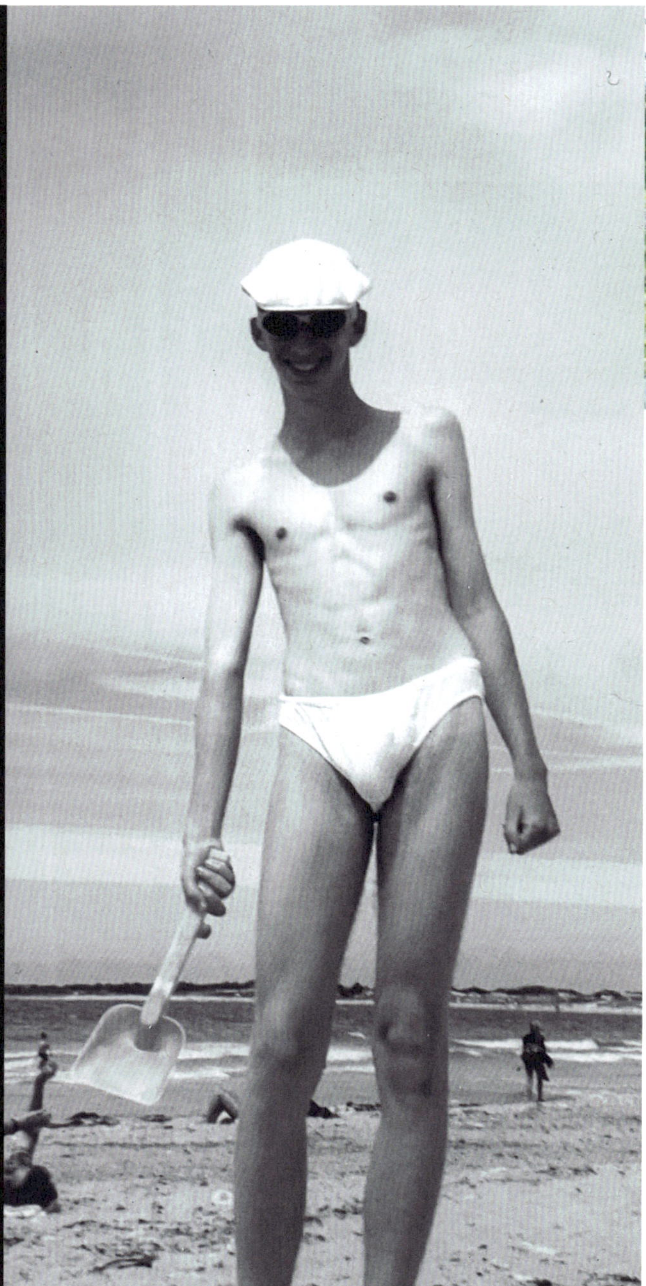

With my friend Gabriel, I had a really good time watching movies like *Dr. No* or *From Russia With Love*. We were into futuristic interior designs and villains with German accents. → 97

So the dress found me, and the first time I put it on was while visiting documenta 10 as a tourist, and it was a big thing for me. → 96

97

HERMANN: We can also jump ahead a bit. This one, for example, is from 1997, the "Best German dance solo" competition at the euro-scene dance and theater festival in Leipzig. Based on an idea of Alain Platel, all kinds of different people would show dance solos on top of a large table, no matter their age, education, or discipline, which excited me. I was 16 and still at school, when I saw the announcement on a flyer, and I applied.

IGOR: But how? I mean, you had to have a title or a description of the work?

HERMANN: There were different elements. For example, a golden dress that I bought in the autumn of 1997, before I knew about this competition.

→ 95

IGOR: How did you get this dress?

HERMANN: I bought it in a second-hand shop during an afternoon in the summer of 1997, probably after school. So the dress found me, and the first time I put it on was while visiting documenta 10 as a tourist, and it was a big thing for me.

IGOR: Okay, what do you mean? You went to documenta in a golden dress?

HERMANN: Yes, it was a visit to documenta 10 with my mother and her boyfriend. We were driving to Kassel by car, and I remember the date, August 31, 1997 because on the radio we listened to the news of Lady Diana's death. And then I thought, I will put on my golden dress from the second-hand shop and put some black color on my eyebrows. I felt an instinctive wish to participate in this art event, even as a tourist. Maybe there was a fantasy: What if I could enter the art field without curators and gatekeepers, just like this?

IGOR: How old were you then?

HERMANN: I was 15, almost 16. Many things were happening simultaneously, like going to record shops, learning to know different styles of electronic music together with my best friend, which was a big discovery. Music was also one element that led me to create this first dance solo in 1997. I chose

Kosma's *Les Promesses D'Une Chevelure*, a kind of 1990s downbeat track that invoked in me a feeling of an imaginary 1960s. At the same moment, I really adored the campness of older James Bond movies. With my friend Gabriel, I had a really good time watching movies like *Dr. No* or *From Russia With Love*. We were into futuristic interior designs and villains with German accents. At that time, in the 1990s, there was this big retro wave going on.

IGOR: Yeah.

HERMANN: And I think that's how the title of this solo in 1997 came into being: *Agent U8—Nizza 1964*. So there were certain constraints for the solo, like the costume, the length of the music, the title. Next, I made myself cues: At certain parts of the music, I would make specific movements or interact with my prop, the rest was mainly improvised. I also didn't know how to rehearse in that sense. I put on a record in my room and then started moving. The hat you can see here in the picture, it came from a house of relatives in West Germany that was still full of different items from the 1950s and 1960s, so I used it for the costume. At the same time, the bag I had as a prop I found in an empty building in Leipzig. In the 1990s, there were lots of these lost places, where we used to go as youngsters to check if there's anything we could find. So this context of the table in 1997 was a point where all these different influences would come together, and for the first time, there was a measure of public exposure. It also marked the discovery of contemporary dance as an art form I would feel driven to.

→ 94

Where I come from, dance was a much less defined territory. That was immensely liberating, I felt. → 105

# 7 KULTUR FÜR ALLE

**Hermann Heisig, 16, Schüler und Spontantänzer:**

**„Hier weiß man nie, wohin die Reise geht"**

Manche sagen, Leipzig wisse nicht genau, wo es hinwolle. Hermann Heisig findet das gar nicht weiter schlimm: „Das schlägt in alle Richtungen aus, und man weiß nie genau, wohin die Reise geht. Dadurch herrscht hier eine sehr lebendige, urbane Atmosphäre." Außerdem sind die Preise für Kulturveranstaltungen konkurrenzlos günstig: Schauspiel, Oper und Museen verschleudern Hochklassiges geradezu. „Was Musik, Theater und Clubs angeht, passiert eine ganze Menge. Die Leute hier machen einfach." Und Hermann macht vor: Beim Tanzwettbewerb des Theaterfestivals euro-scene überraschte er letztes Jahr mit vielbejubelten Spontanauftritten außerhalb der Konkurrenz. Einfach, weil er Lust dazu hatte. Ein anderes Beispiel ist das Brockdorf Klanglabor, in dem Hermann ebenfalls mitmischt: Ein paar junge Leute organisieren kuriose „Parties mit künstlerischem Anspruch" – zuletzt in der Wahlnacht des 27. September vor laufenden MDR-Kameras im Maga Pon.

"ten reasons to love Leipzig", Kreuzer Magazine

19

# 98

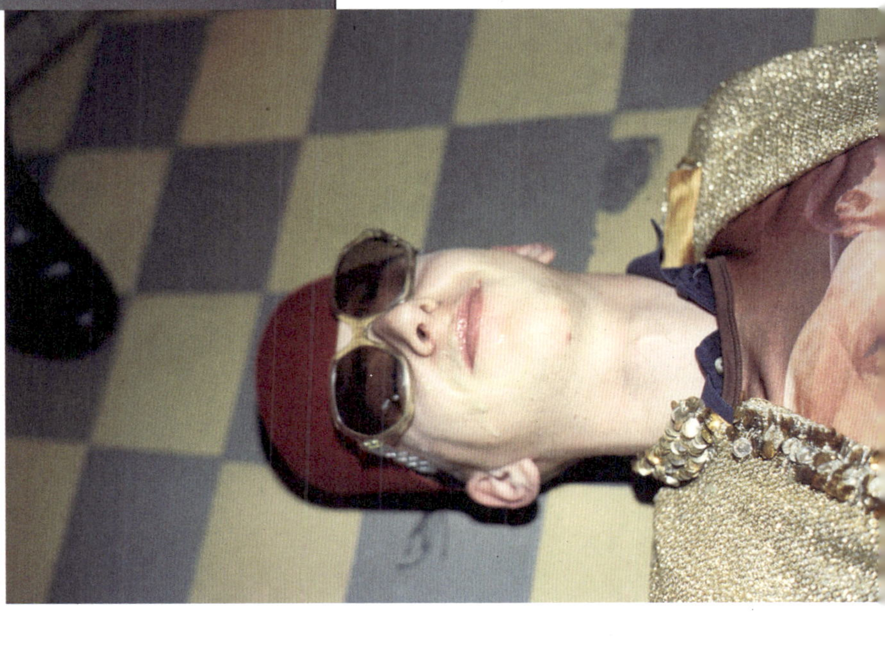

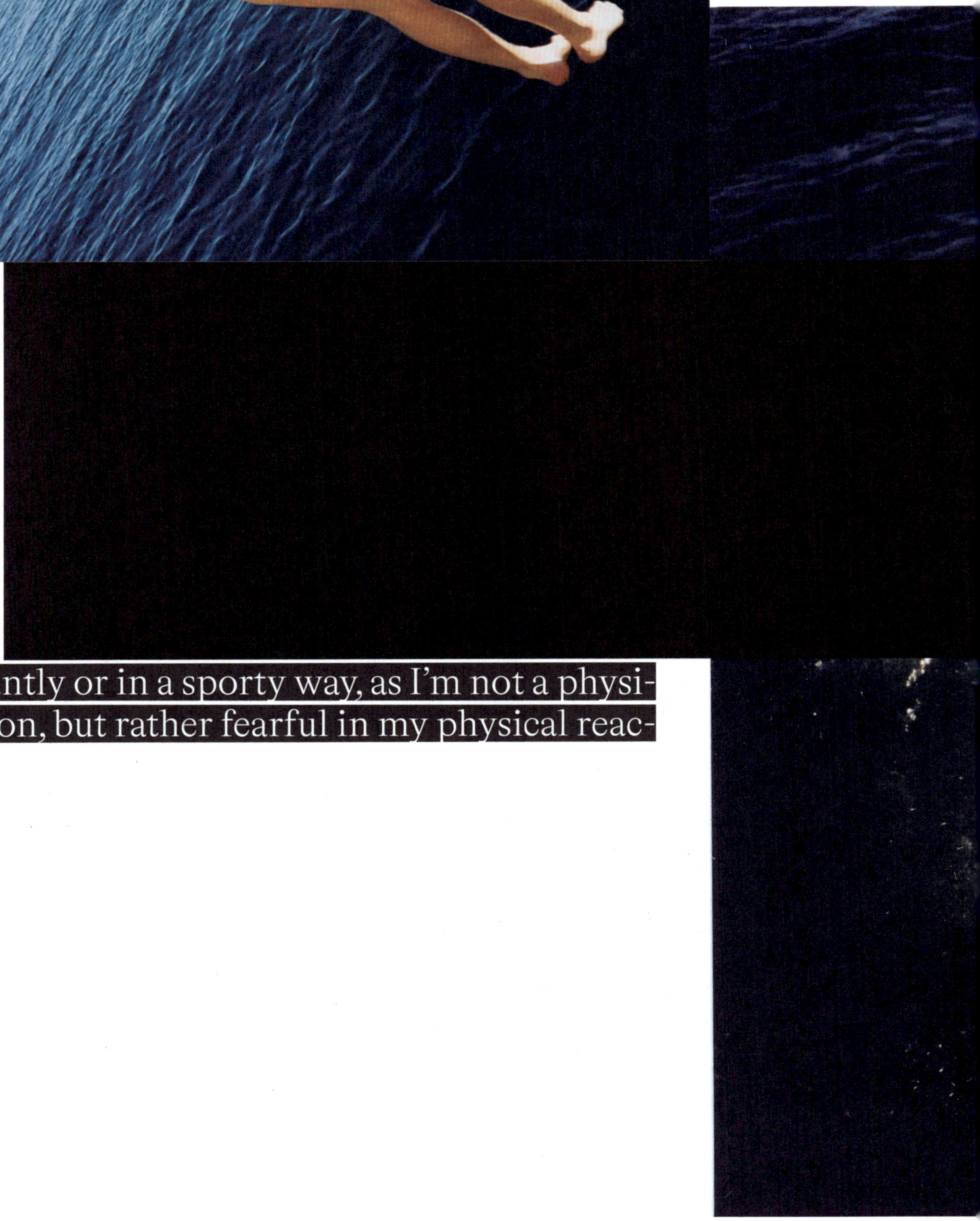

I'm not jumping elegantly or in a sporty way, as I'm not a physically courageous person, but rather fearful in my physical reactions. → 104

→ 102

HERMANN: This picture was actually taken around the same time, in 1998, a photo from a holiday.
IGOR: Why this picture?
HERMANN: It is me jumping into the water, I chose it intuitively … **I'm not jumping elegantly or in a sporty way, as I'm not a physically courageous person, but rather fearful in my physical reactions.**
IGOR: As opposed to being like a "fish in the water"—
HERMANN: As I said before, as a teenager, I rejected sports, all this idea of competition, following rules … But with dance and performance, I was thinking, oh wow, maybe that's a way to transform my relationship to physicality.
IGOR: The notion of the "lanky body". The awkward, disproportional body—
HERMANN: Choosing this holiday picture, I also thought, you know, it's simply an act of jumping into the water. Yet, within this act, there is something about a shift between elements, in this case from air to water. And on the way, potentially getting transformed. There is something very basic about it. And still, there is a certain clumsiness in the way you encounter another entity or another person. Later, in dance education, I encountered this a lot in contact improvisation: how to take the weight when it comes at you. As a tall person, I didn't have a stable relationship with the ground. It's difficult for a tall body to hold someone or even go down to lift someone. It's just a longer way down and up. And I was fascinated by this aspect, "to become friends with the floor", as a dance teacher later put it. To practice this, to address these topics for my body, was a bit of an impossible task. But, uh, I felt attracted to this impossibility, and I wanted to work with it.
IGOR: I assume that it has to do with the notion of clumsiness as a way of being, which can also be affirmed rather than sanctioned as something bad. The comic spirit of inclusion …

HERMANN: It's interesting you should mention this—also next to the "fish in water." It reminds me of Henri Bergson's essay on laughter and the meaning of the comic. It was first published in 1900, and I used it as a source for *Slap/Stick*, a solo I created in 2013, when I became a father for the first time. In this text, Bergson describes the comic in a very physical way. For example, he writes about the situation of a person looking into the air without noticing a stone and stumbling over it — the inability to adapt to the "fluidity of life" as an endless source of comedy.

IGOR: Hm.

HERMANN: And since I started to engage with contemporary dance and performance, this comic aspect has been following me—the image of a funny dancer, a funny performer. And I am constantly undecided about how to react to this—whether I should escape or rather embrace it. Working with the element of comedy easily implies a certain devaluation of the artistic work; it is not really "taken seriously," especially in Germany with its traditional division of serious art versus entertainment. But anyway, escape does not really feel possible, as the comical is something I am instinctively drawn to. I love the intersection between comedy and anarchy, and this very delicate zone between intended and unintended comedy. So, jumping back to the end of the 1990s, I clumsily started taking modern dance training once or twice a week with a former ballerina of the Leipzig Opera, Heike Bastian. And at least for where I come from, dance was a much less defined territory. That was immensely liberating, I felt.

→ 98

Sometimes it was quite schizophrenic. I would go to a party at night, receiving a stamp on my hand at the entrance. And then, the next morning, I would go to serve in church. And when holding my hand in a praying position, the stamp of the party from the previous night was revealed. → 108

# 1999

Loveparade 1999:
Music is the key

Events by
Brockdorff Klang Labor
were more of an
anarchic space

IGOR: But how did your interest continue after 1997?
HERMANN: Through the solo on the table, I got to know an artist collective called Brockdorff Klang Labor. They would organize self-made happenings somewhere in between concert, performance and party, starting in the empty flat below the apartment they were living in. In the 1990s, most of the industry in Leipzig had collapsed, and around 100,000 people were leaving the city. There was lots of empty space, either abandoned factories or apartment buildings, in which maybe only one or two flats would still be inhabited and the rest empty. This benefited a certain type of culture, for example, my friends from Brockdorff Klang Labor. For their events, they invited me to create solo dances. I was 16, and they were about 25.
IGOR: Really? So they were much older?
HERMANN: Yes. I was super happy about this invitation, as it gave me the possibility to continue a practice of improvising dances in self-organized environments, in direct contact with the public.
IGOR: So they invited you to be part of their happenings?
HERMANN: Exactly. The events by Brockdorff Klang Labor were more of an anarchic space. A bit like in this picture. This action was called *Geheimnisse der Transsexualität*, and we would perform with printed-out pictures of vulvae and penises. I put it here, next to this picture of my confirmation in a Catholic church.

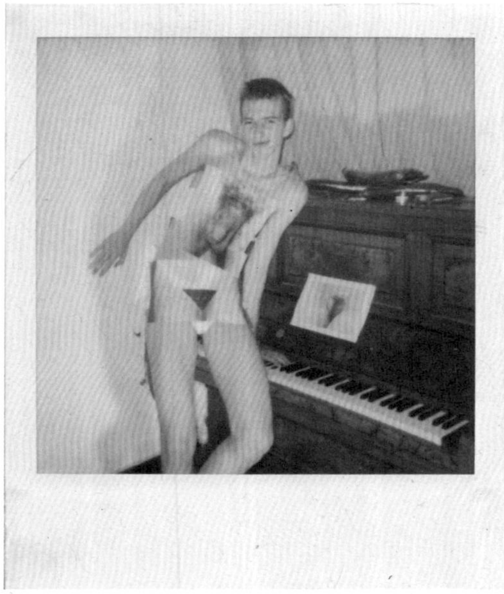

→ 107

IGOR: Did you go through the church rituals?
HERMANN: Yes. I was an altar boy at Catholic mass for many years. So sometimes it was quite schizophrenic. I would go to a party at night, receiving a stamp on my hand at the entrance. And then, the next morning, I would go to serve in church. And when holding my hand in a praying position, the stamp of the party from the previous night was revealed.

IGOR: And how do you feel about this contradiction now? What is your stand on religion?

HERMANN: Um—I would consider myself religious.

IGOR: Thank you for sharing that. I mean, because I guessed somehow. That's also interesting.

HERMANN: I'm a member of the Catholic Church, and I keep that connection, although I don't attend church often. Last summer I went to Assisi as a tourist, and in the Basilica I attended mass for the first time in many years. In Berlin, I never go. Because, of course, on the other hand, there is so much rigidity within Catholicism. Just like in the picture. This is the bishop from the front, and my friend's mother being a mentor of sorts from the back, putting her arm on my shoulder, encouraging me from the back.

→ 106

IGOR: It's like becoming an adult—

HERMANN: Yes. After this, you become, let's say, a full member of the church. There is a very weird relationship to performance in all of this.

IGOR: **Catholicism is super theatrical.**

HERMANN: And sometimes it's hilarious, as nothing is supposed to go wrong in the ritual, which of course happens many times. I was an altar boy until I turned 18.

→ 62

IGOR: So you were doing all those performance acts with an anarchist art collective while being still an altar boy in the Catholic Church?

HERMANN: Yes, and partly I also enjoyed the contrast of slipping from one world into the other. And lately, I have been thinking a lot about religion again, what it can do, and what it can provide.

# 1999

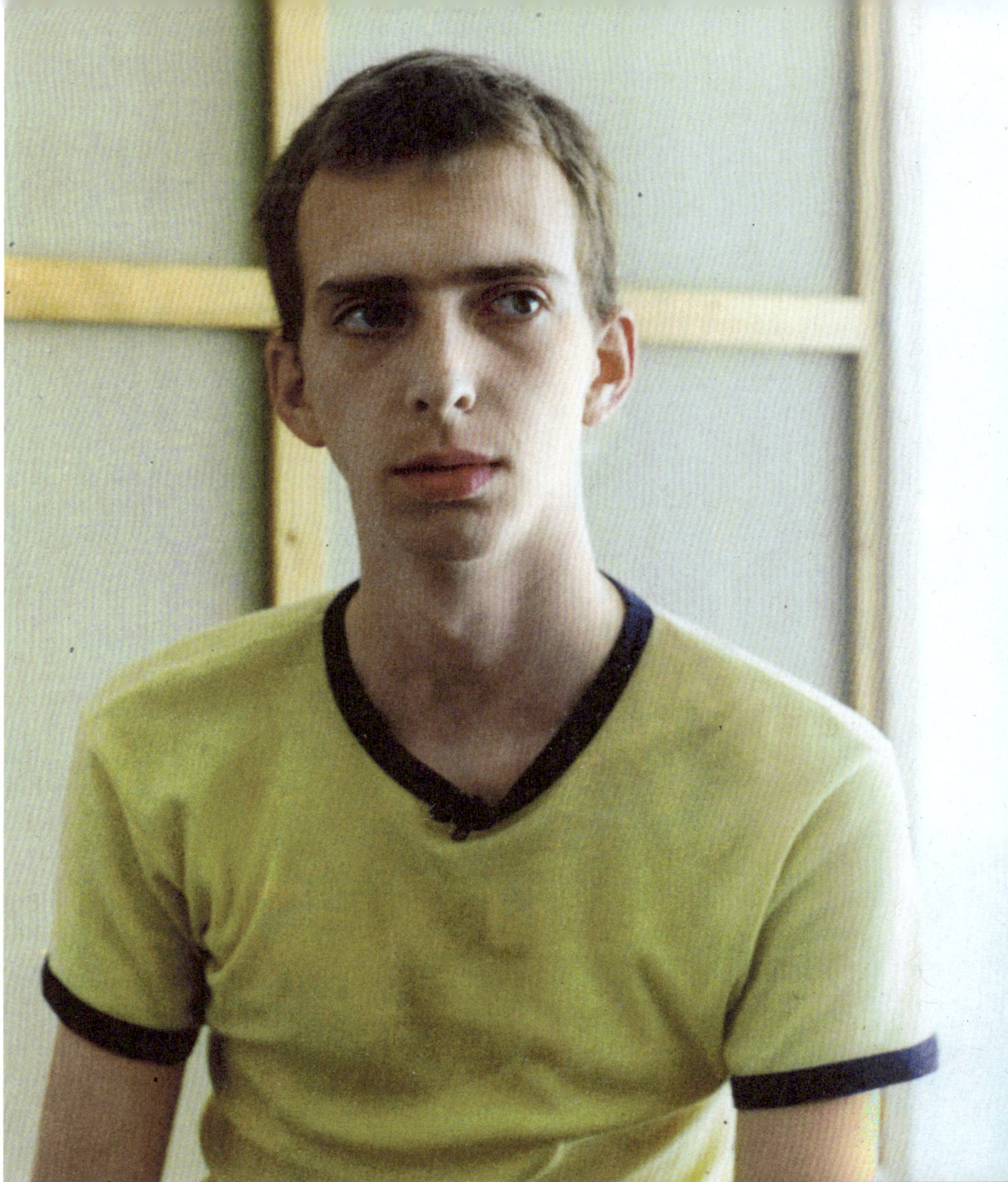

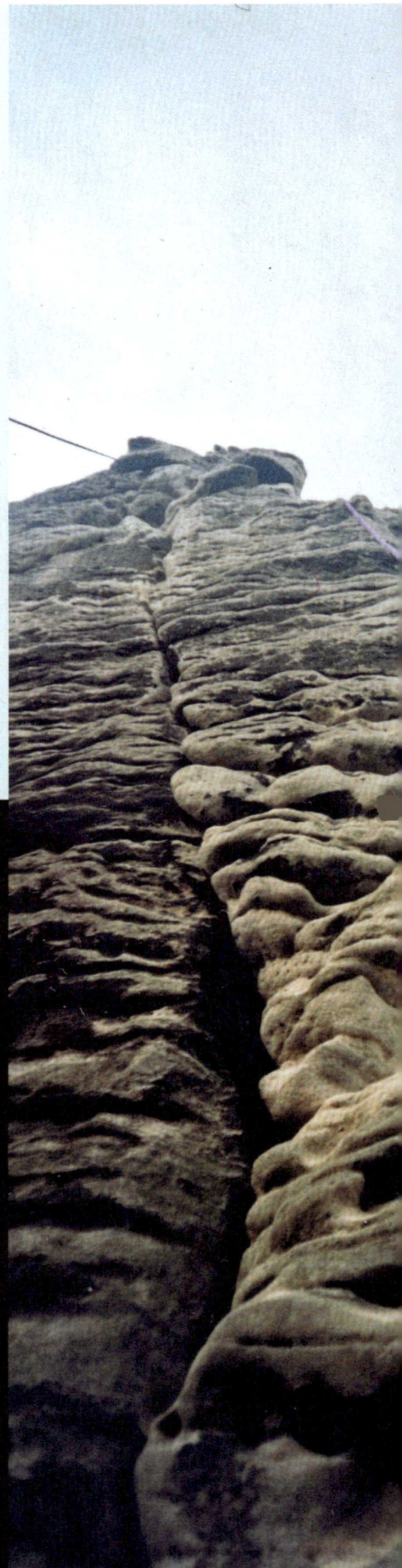

# 20

# 20

# 20

Being suddenly confronted with assisting elderly people, cleaning the place, preparing meals, and having to be efficient in time, it was quite a difference compared to my life before. → 120

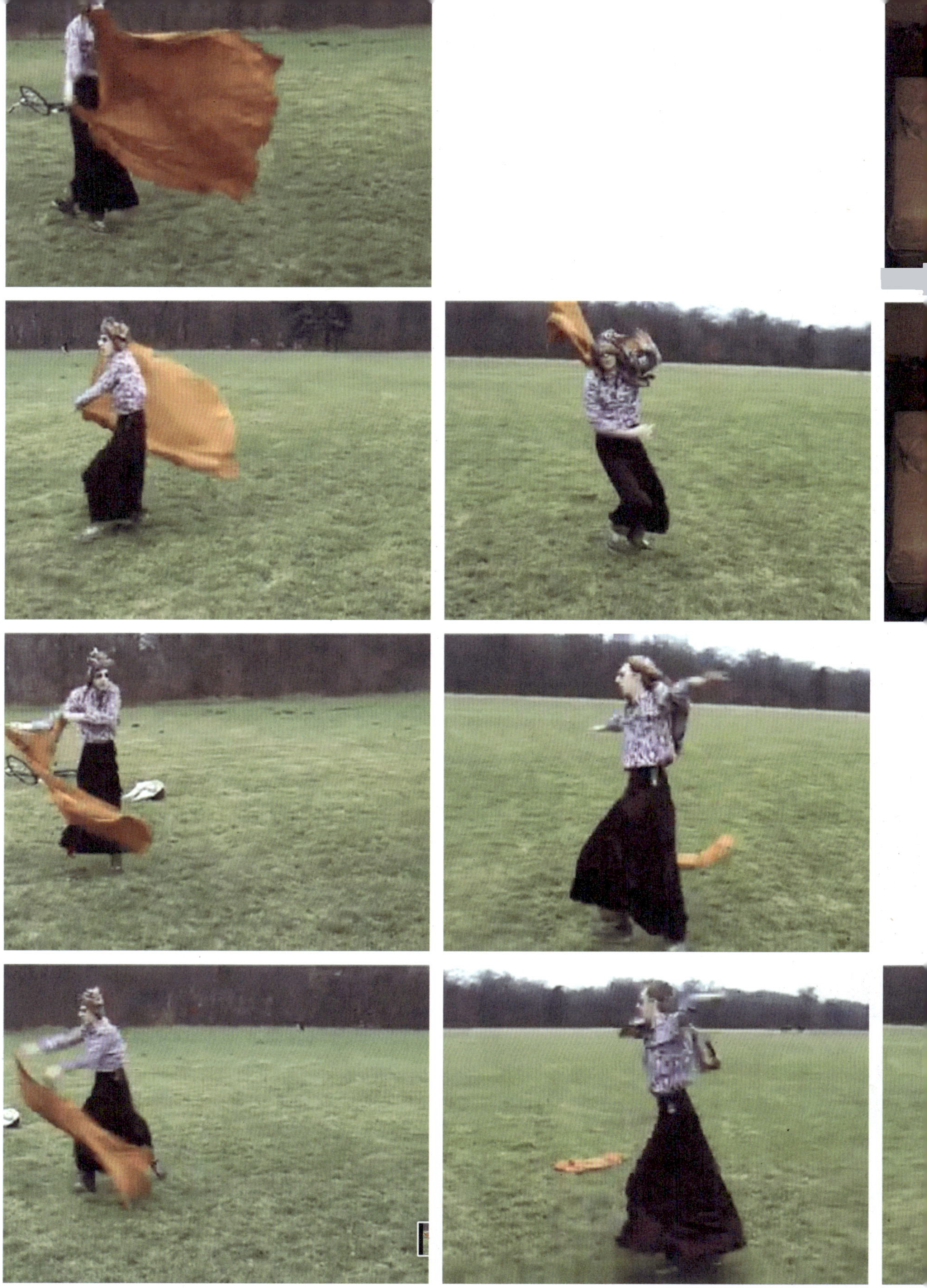

# 2001

"Zimmer 707 & die Bewohner"
Hotel Holiday Inn
euro-scene leipzig

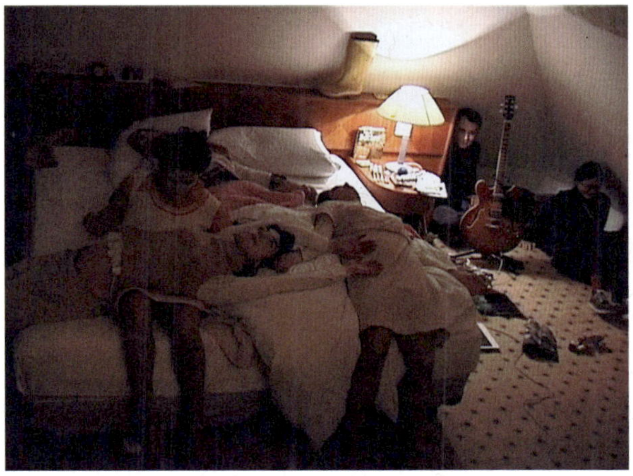

→ 112

IGOR: I will jump pictures. Why this one?

HERMANN: Oh! For me, it represents the year 2000. Moving to Berlin. Wanting to do things with dance but not exactly knowing how to do it.

IGOR: But you were determined at that time that this is what you're going to do?

HERMANN: I mean, it was coming in waves. These thoughts: what to do if it doesn't work? Around 2002, 2003 and 2004, I was auditioning for many dance schools, and I failed. SNDO in Amsterdam, for example; SEAD in Salzburg; EDDC in Arnhem.

IGOR: You tried to enter all these schools?

HERMANN: Yes, and also P.A.R.T.S. in Brussels. At the same time, in 2002, I started dance training at a private school in Kreuzberg, Die Etage.

IGOR: But have you been discouraged by these failures?

HERMANN: It was a complex time. But retrospectively, I am very thankful that I stayed in Berlin in the end. At this moment, there was much less economic pressure in Berlin, allowing me to try things out. I had a part-time job that earned me a little bit of money. I had refused mandatory army service; as a conscientious objector, I started working as a geriatric nurse in a flat where six elderly women with Alzheimer's disease lived together. First for a year in 2000 and 2001, and later I continued this as a side job on weekends. I would live in my father's place; there was no rent to pay, so I would have a little bit of money to see shows, go out to dance, have a coffee here and there, go to training. And after my social service finished in 2001, I decided to stay in Berlin, as I knew there was much more to discover.

IGOR: And how was that, taking care of the Alzheimer's ladies?

→ 116

HERMANN: It was quite a reality check. **Being suddenly confronted with assisting elderly people, cleaning the place, preparing meals, and having to be efficient in time, it was quite a difference compared to my life before.** And of course, it was a challenge for me to be in a new city, being much more anonymous. In Leipzig, everything was more comfortable because I was a little bit known in the cultural field.

IGOR: Yeah, yeah, yeah.

HERMANN: But on the other hand, Leipzig remained close by; I could always go back and forth, so I could use that a little bit. Through performing there, I would get to know other dancers and performers working in Berlin. So, bit by bit, I could expand my network in Berlin as well, building relations that would enable me to continue. In 2004, for example, through a friend in Leipzig, I got to know Anja Müller. I would perform in her piece *Klar Sicht* in *Tanztage* at Sophiensæle in Berlin, curated by Barbara Friedrich at the time. Places like *Tanztage* were windows of opportunity for gaining visibility; a kind of permeability that is now much less happening in Berlin.

IGOR: What do you mean by permeability?

HERMANN: I mean uncomplicated opportunities that allow you to enter the artistic field, learning by doing.

IGOR: Yeah, yeah, yeah.

HERMANN: For example, places like Dock 11 in Kastanienallee. They knew me only a little when I approached them in 2005 with my friend and collaborator Marina Quesada, asking them to present a first full-length performance there, *Abhanden kommen/die Landschaft*, which was inspired by working with Alzheimer's and dementia patients. Kirsten Seeligmüller and Wibke Janssen gave us a slot in their program without checking too much on us beforehand. And through producing this work, other things became possible. I don't want to be too pessimistic, but in contemporary Berlin, things have become much more competitive, and these windows of opportunity are much smaller.

→ 136

IGOR: The need to build a career.

HERMANN: Or the other way round: without these openings, there is an increasing impossibility of building a career.

A first apartment
Lychener Str. 64, Berlin Prenzlauer Berg
80,80 sqm / 370,48 €

HEISIG * METTKE

# 20

"Kompott zweier Einquartierender with Marina Quesada in a shopwindow Oranienstr., Kreuzberg

# 02

only one fashion shooting so far:
style and the family tunes, Tresor Berlin

performing in the booth of edition sutstein,
Leipzig Book Fair,

# 2003

Through working on
"Zimmer 707 & die Bewohner"
in 2001, I got to know
media artist and
performative urbanist
Diana Wesser

In 2003, she invited Marina Quesada and me
to take part in "das Hochzeitsfest",
a site specific work in Halle-Neustadt
one of the largest GDR urban planning projects

20

Meine Sybille!

Unfallstelle Sybille

03

For two weeks we were around in public space, embodying a fictional couple, Helmut and Sybille… preparing an artificial marriage of the two characters by asking people for rituals to celebrate.

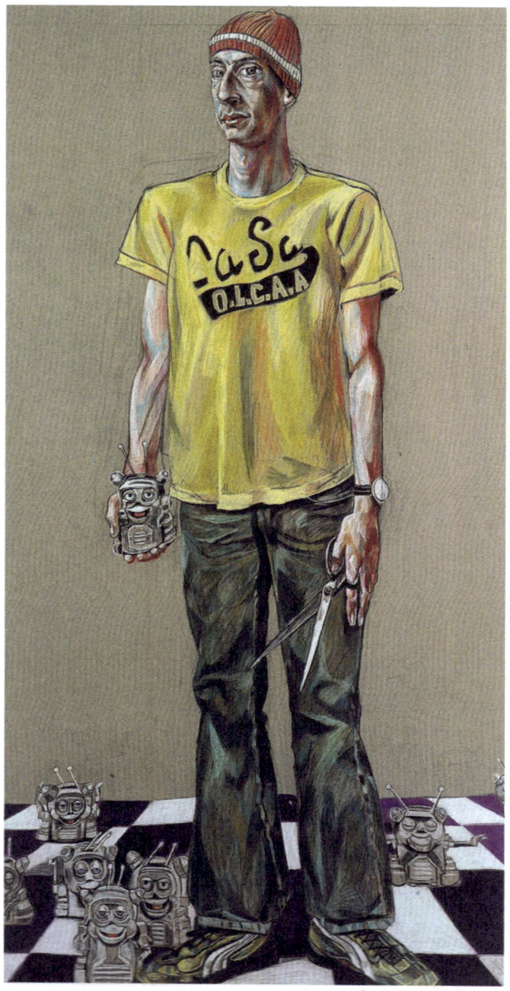


Portrait as Part of the series "Berliner Sittengemälde" ANTOINETTE

**IGOR:** And how was the private school experience?

**HERMANN:** Not that easy! The school was called "Die Etage", it was located in Kreuzberg. I had a number of dance classes each day, like ballet, modern dance, Graham, some Cunningham—and I had the feeling it was a place that struggled with the fact that it was not a renowned art school. As students, we didn't feel we were taken seriously.
On the other hand, the Etage was also a place where I met some very important people for me, for example Thomas Proksch, a friend, artistic partner and roommate for many years, ... Marina Quesada, with whom I developed my very first collaborative works ... and last but not least Anne Zacho Søgaard, we have been a couple since 2006.

**IGOR:** Was Anne in the same school?

**HERMANN:** Yes, Die Etage consisted of different departments: an Acting department where Anne studied, Thomas was in the Pantomime department, I was in Dance, and there were Stage Design and Acrobatics too. You were paying to attend the school—actually, half of the fees were paid by my grandmother from the mother's side, the other half by my father, in total around €300 a month.

**IGOR:** So you had the support of your grandmother?

**HERMANN:** Yes, and I am very thankful as she supported me although I think she didn't fully understand why it was my wish to do this education.

**IGOR:** But what was your parent's relation to what you were doing?

**HERMANN:** My father often said he would see me more as somebody who likes to write, likes history, a bit of a dreamy person—

**IGOR:** So, have you been brainy?

**HERMANN:** I mean, I work a lot through imagination today as well. Not to do this brain/body separation, but—I like stories. I like history. That was something very strong in my childhood that stays with me. A lot of what happened with dancing came as a surprise to my parents.

IGOR: But how was dance education as an experience to be put through?
HERMANN: It was not easy for me, but Klein Technique, for example, was quite a revelation.
IGOR: So that was something you enjoyed? And what was difficult?
HERMANN: Jazz Dance. Although I have a weird fascination for its performativity ... and Ballet, for sure. It was physically complicated, and on top I didn't like the idea of it. On the other hand, after about two and a half years, I started to have a slight feeling of joy. I felt my body changing a little. I felt an ability to perceive space differently and being able to memorize movements. And I thought: it's this that you have to learn—what is not easy for you.

→ 133

IGOR: So in a way, craft entered the story.
HERMANN: I wanted to go through these processes.
IGOR: What is your relation to craft?
HERMANN: I like the idea of working with repetition, repeating some operation and becoming better at it, gradually finding "your" way of doing things.
IGOR: Yeah, appropriation is related to repetition as well.
HERMANN: I come from improvising, and I felt I needed another consciousness about dealing with time and space, in a way. And to be able to say, okay, I do a piece, depending not only on what I am doing but also on the whole apparatus, the light, for example.
IGOR: So that's what I'm asking you. When you say that you started making performances I assume you meant taking into account the whole stage apparatus.
HERMANN: Well, it's not that my interest is completely limited on creating works for the black box ... as there is this desire from the start to deal with spaces not necessarily made for performing—but there was a feeling like: basically I have to learn to know the theatre and how it works.

# 2004

Die Etage would offer classes only from around 10.00 to 16.00, so after there was time and space ~~to work with in collaboration~~ to rehearse, kind of self-learning how to create performance

I felt an ability to perceive space differently and being able to memorize movements. And I thought: it's this that you have to learn—what is not easy for you. → 131

RIEN
NEVA
PLUS!
WDR
MILES
OSCAR PETERSON

# 2004

NEWSFLASH with dearest
Anne Zacho Søgaard

For example, places like Dock 11 in Kastanienallee. They knew me only a little when I approached them in 2005 with my friend and collaborator Marina Quesada, asking them to present a first full-length performance there, *Abhanden kommen/ die Landschaft*, which was inspired by working with Alzheimer's and dementia patients. They gave us a slot in their program without checking too much on us beforehand. And through producing this work, other things became possible. → 121

20

performing in
"Dancing about Architecture"
by Diana Wesser

05

# 200

Schloss Lanke, a place I would rehearse
in the summer of 2005..
An example of interim use of an
empty building for artistic purposes.
Later, it was turned into apartments.

# 25

*Randshow* in summer 2006, a wandering performance bypassing the periphery between Berlin and Copenhagen, which Anne and I initiated together. → 142

20

# 06

→ 145

→ 145

HERMANN: This is a bit of an interlude. These pictures I took in 2006. **The demolition of certain communist buildings.** For example, this is Palast der Republik in Berlin, I was accidentally passing by with my bike and I took a picture. And as well, here, this is the Karl Marx relief at the University of Leipzig. I also accidentally passed by when it was pulled down. Both places have a history of socialism destroying former structures, the old Berlin Palace, the university church in Leipzig—and then, in 2006, these socialist structures were again demolished to make space for different forms of reconstruction.
IGOR: But you did some site specific work there?
HERMANN: No, I was just documenting this for myself. But I chose these pictures, as there is something about a condition in the 2000s within eastern Germany. A struggle about identity, trying to un-do socialist traces, actually destroying traces of history in order to invent a new version of the past.
And because you mentioned site-specific work—this picture here is the ***Randshow* in summer 2006, a wandering performance bypassing the periphery between Berlin and Copenhagen, which Anne and I initiated together.** After finishing my dance education in the spring of 2006, I had a lot of joy researching this project, drifting through the landscape and discovering a route through six different places in northeastern Germany and the south of Denmark.
A bit later, in August 2006, as a group of eight artists, we were traveling along this route from one spot to another, for three weeks. In each place, we would stay for three days, creating a site-specific work in collaboration with a local artist or artist group. This, for example, was in Dargun in Mecklenburg, an old castle that has been in ruins since 1945. At that spot, we contacted a folk dance group, asking them if they would want to perform with us. The idea was that they would teach us some of their folk dances, and we would teach them some choreography of ours in

return. Out of this we would develop a performance in the ruin of Dargun Castle. Later, the footage of this dance became a music video for my friends Brockdorff Klang Labor from Leipzig.

IGOR: But how was this funded?

HERMANN: It was one of the first times I applied for funding. For example, for *Randshow,* I remember a grant of 4000 Euro by Fonds Darstellende Künste, and then, miraculously, I managed to obtain 700 Euro from the Ministry of Education in Mecklenburg-Vorpommern; I forgot how. We were eight people on the road for three weeks. I remember that at the end, each of us had a salary of about 350 Euro for everything.

IGOR: This is when it starts, applications.

HERMANN: Yes. For example, for *Abhanden kommen/die Landschaft* 2005 in Dock 11, I remember as well a grant of 4000 € in total by the local authority in Prenzlauer Berg, Kulturamt Pankow. With these 4000 €, Marina Quesada and I did a quintet, including us as performers. Each one of us received maybe 400 or €500 for two months of work. This was also Berlin in the 00s: self-exploitation at its best! We were organizing an audition for that piece. And then twenty people showed up, dancers who had finished their academies while my friend Marina and I were still in dance education, but we were the directors of the project. It was quite demanding, but also a big learning-by-doing process.

# 30

In 2006, I joined my grandfather on a trip to Wrocław, and although I felt he initially rejected any emotionality towards revisiting the city, it was important for us to be there together. → 31

The demolition of certain communist buildings. → 142

06

# 20

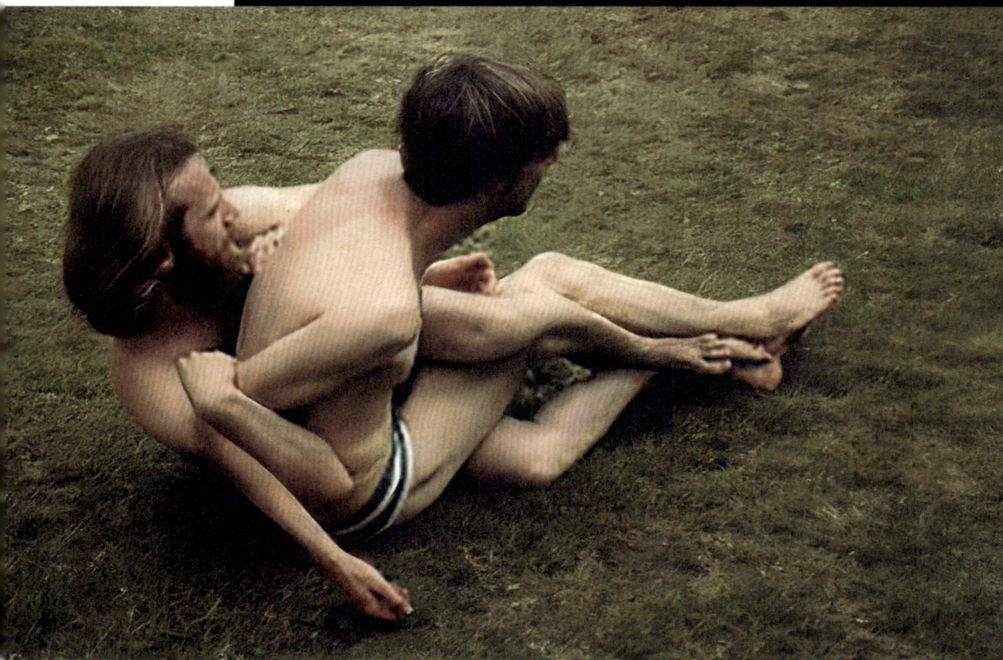

*ex.e.r.ce 07*, a seven-month program for choreography at CCN Montpellier. → 150

# 07

# 20

*Movements of Lindenau*, created in Leipzig in collaboration with Diana Wesser, just after my return from Montpellier in autumn 2007. It's a performance based on walks through Lindenau, a quarter in the west of Leipzig with a strong industrial past. → 151

# 07

→ 146

IGOR: So, after finishing your training in Berlin, you went to France?

HERMANN: Yes, doing *ex.e.r.ce 07*, a seven-month program for choreography at CCN Montpellier. This is a funny Polaroid with Xavier le Roy, our teacher and mentor there. He was a great inspiration for me, for many reasons, but also because, in a way, he is another lanky body! Studying molecular biology, playing basketball—attending dance classes in France in the early 1990s, being a stranger to this training. But then his strategy to get out of this was very different.

IGOR: Yeah, an interesting example of how to negotiate your place in dance.

HERMANN: Xavier was invited to be artist-in-residence for two years at CCN Montpellier, which was directed by Mathilde Monnier at the time. And so, in 2007, they both directed this course for seven months with fourteen students from different places and from different disciplines.

IGOR: How was that?

HERMANN: It was quite mind-blowing. At first it felt a bit like a movie. A few years earlier, at the Berlinale, Anne and I had seen a documentary about Mathilde Monnier, *Vers Mathilde* by Claire Denis. And to be at CCN Montpellier and have Mathilde as a teacher along with Xavier, Jonathan Burrows or Mark Tompkins was a bit like a dream. All of a sudden, I was thrown into this very inspiring institution and learned of entirely new approaches to making work and reflecting on it together. And suddenly you feel the situation around you changing, how the market would start to think of you as someone potentially interesting.

IGOR: The situation changed because of following that program?

HERMANN: Partly, yes, I think. The institution's recognition in choosing you to be a student there opens other doors. In the summer of 2007, after finishing the *ex.er.ce* program, we as students were invited to do something in *Tanz im August* in Berlin. We collectively organized KAF, *Knowledge and Fun,* a two-week program of learning, exchanging and performing in HAU 3. It was a huge learning process on many levels.

IGOR: And I want to know what this picture is about—

HERMANN: This is *Movements of Lindenau,* created in Leipzig in collaboration with Diana Wesser, just after my return from Montpellier in autumn 2007. It's a performance based on walks through Lindenau, a quarter in the west of Leipzig with a strong industrial past. Diana and I created two performances related to this place, one in 2007 and one in 2017. In 2007, that area was still marked by many empty and run-down buildings. And this is me in 2017, in the same spot. It's a work about visiting and re-visiting a spot, observing processes of change.

→ 111

IGOR: So there is a continuous preoccupation with the public space throughout your artistic work.

HERMANN: I would say so.

IGOR: But why is there an interest in going out, into public space?

HERMANN: I'm very inspired by places—physically experiencing and perceiving their structure, their boundaries. Definitely, I have been influenced by growing up in Leipzig in the 1990s, a city in dramatic transformation. We mentioned it before: whole industries broke away, and around 100,000 inhabitants left the city. As a teenager, this transition made a big mark on me, and in the 1990s, it was very common to enter empty houses, for partying purposes, but also just to meander through abandoned space. When Diana Wesser and I worked on *Lindenau Revisited* in 2017, the situation in Leipzig had already flipped. In the years after 2010, Leipzig started to grow again very quickly, so now there is a housing problem. Less space, which creates a very different way of being in the city.

# 20

in this beautif-
Countryside
Tanztage Berlin

# 08

In 2006, during *mobile academy* in Warsaw, I met Meg Stuart, whose work was super inspiring. Seeing *ALIBI* in 2001 was a big eye-opener for me. At the end of 2007, she invited me to work with her as a performer, and I happily said yes. → 158

performing in "Die Maßnahme / Mauser" by Frank Castorf & Meg Stuart after Brecht & Müller, Volksbühne am Rosa-Luxemburg-Platz, Berlin

# 20

# 08

At different moments, be it in 2002 or 2016, the classic question would come up: „But am I able to make a living out of this?“ → 174

Pongo Land, collaborating with Nuno Lucas

2009

Performing in
"one shared object PROFIT AND LOSS"
by Martin Nachbar and Martine Pisani

IGOR: It is around that time—2007, 2008, 2009—when I noticed you. Because I came to Berlin from time to time, and I had this strange feeling that you were on your way up. There was something around you during that period, an air of expectation. I was seeing you in passing, but I had this strange experience without knowing who you are. Which poses the question: How important is it for you to be recognized?

HERMANN: I mean, I was enjoying it.

IGOR: But in what sense? As a self-image?

HERMANN: It was a certain relief after a longer, harder time of constantly operating with doubts about whether it was the right choice to go into dancing and performing. And then, within a relatively short amount of time, seemingly by magic, things turn, and suddenly, you are at a party during a dance festival and a lot of people want to talk to you. And I had this skill for small talk in artistic contexts. I acquired it as an only child in the 1990s, during exhibition openings of my father, uncle or grandfather. I felt comfortable socializing, connecting with people. But this increase in recognition was also creating new problems.

IGOR: What problems?

HERMANN: Uh, for example, having to choose the right steps. I remember 2008 and 2009 as years when a lot of things overlapped. In July 2007, I returned from Montpellier to Berlin, and a bit earlier, in 2006, during *mobile academy* in Warsaw, I met Meg Stuart, whose work was super inspiring. Seeing *ALIBI* in 2001 was a big eye-opener for me. At the end of 2007, she invited me to work with her as a performer, and I happily said yes. At the same time, I started to do my own work, which got more recognition than before. I started collaborating with my dear friend Nuno Lucas, whom I met during *ex.e.r.ce* in Montpellier, and we created *Pongo Land* as a collaboration in 2008. So I was super happy about that as well. Then, at the beginning of 2009, Meg proposed for me to

→ 153

be part of a mentorship initiative initiated by the Spielart festival in Munich. She would be a mentor, I would be the mentee, and there was a budget of 30,000 Euro that I could create a piece with. And then I also fell into this trap: okay, now I have to do a group piece, to use this window of opportunity as a potential entrance into the bigger European festival circuit.

IGOR: So this is how it works. The art market.

HERMANN: And I was saying yes to too many people.

IGOR: But isn't that a weakness for an artist? Wanting to say yes to everything?

HERMANN: It's generally a problem I have.

IGOR: For building a career, certainly. Yes.

HERMANN: It's an obstacle I would put up myself. But on the other hand—

IGOR: It's also opening you to chance, intuition and the spirit.

HERMANN: I mean, many things were in the air at that time. And I think I also had this idea of single authorship in my mind, perhaps inspired by my father and grandfather from the father's side, being successful authors of their own artistic work. So I was choosing to make a piece for four performers, choreographing it from the outside. I wanted to do things very low-hierarchy, but at the same time to be the author. So it was already complex.

IGOR: There is a contradiction. The tension between collaboration and authorship.

HERMANN: And I wanted to make it work. I felt a pressure to come up with "good decisions". But funnily, now looking at the phots from 2009, I start to like the work. It was called *Themselves already hop!*, a piece on the idea of multitasking, and that is what I was literally doing in 2009.

→ 160

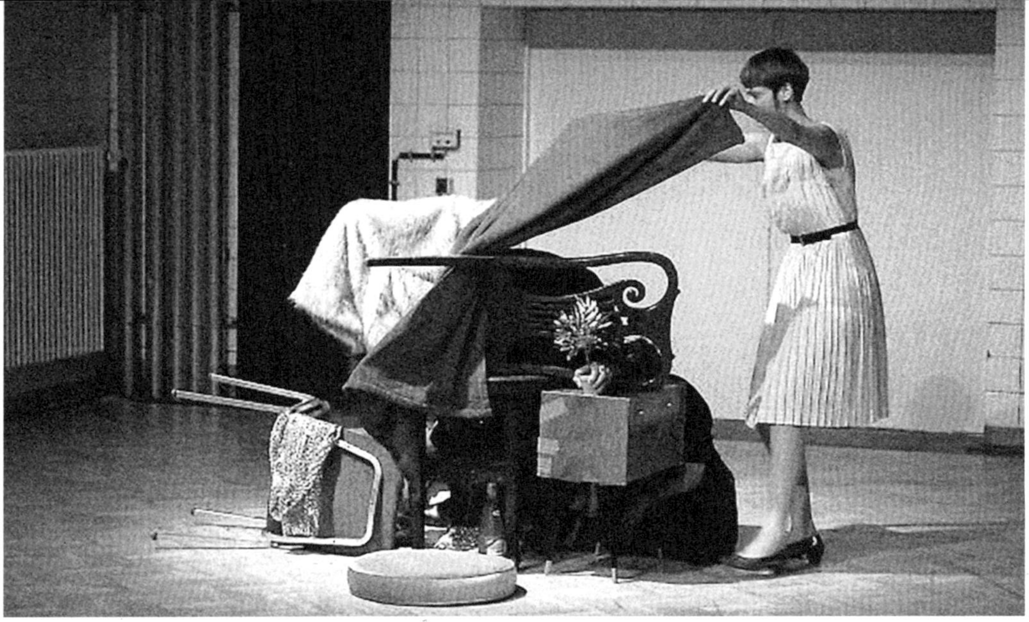

*Themselves already hop!*, a piece on the idea of multitasking, and that is what I was literally doing in 2009. → 159

meeting the objects of my maternal grandparents, after they passed away, Leipzig, Primavesistr. 8

2009

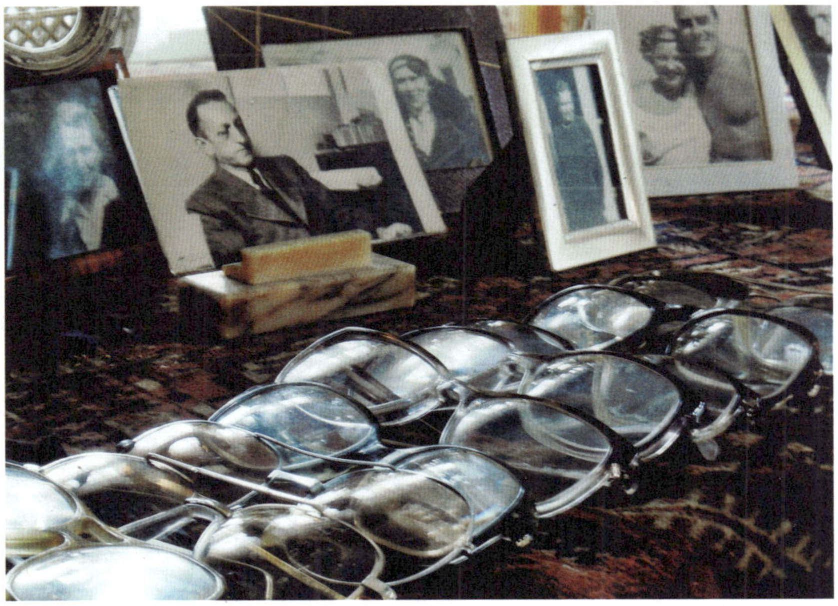

# 20

Schönhauser Allee 44
seen from the outside

A very nice flat, 140 square meters for 626 Euros a month, but heated with coal stoves. It was cold in the winter but fantastic in the summer because of its high ceilings. We hosted so many parties! And a lot of people from the performing arts field passed through this place, living there for a number of weeks or sometimes for years. → 190

# 10

reconstructing the shape of a
vanished department store:
KAUFHAUS URY, during play! Leipzig Festival

20

research research research, fabrik Potsdam

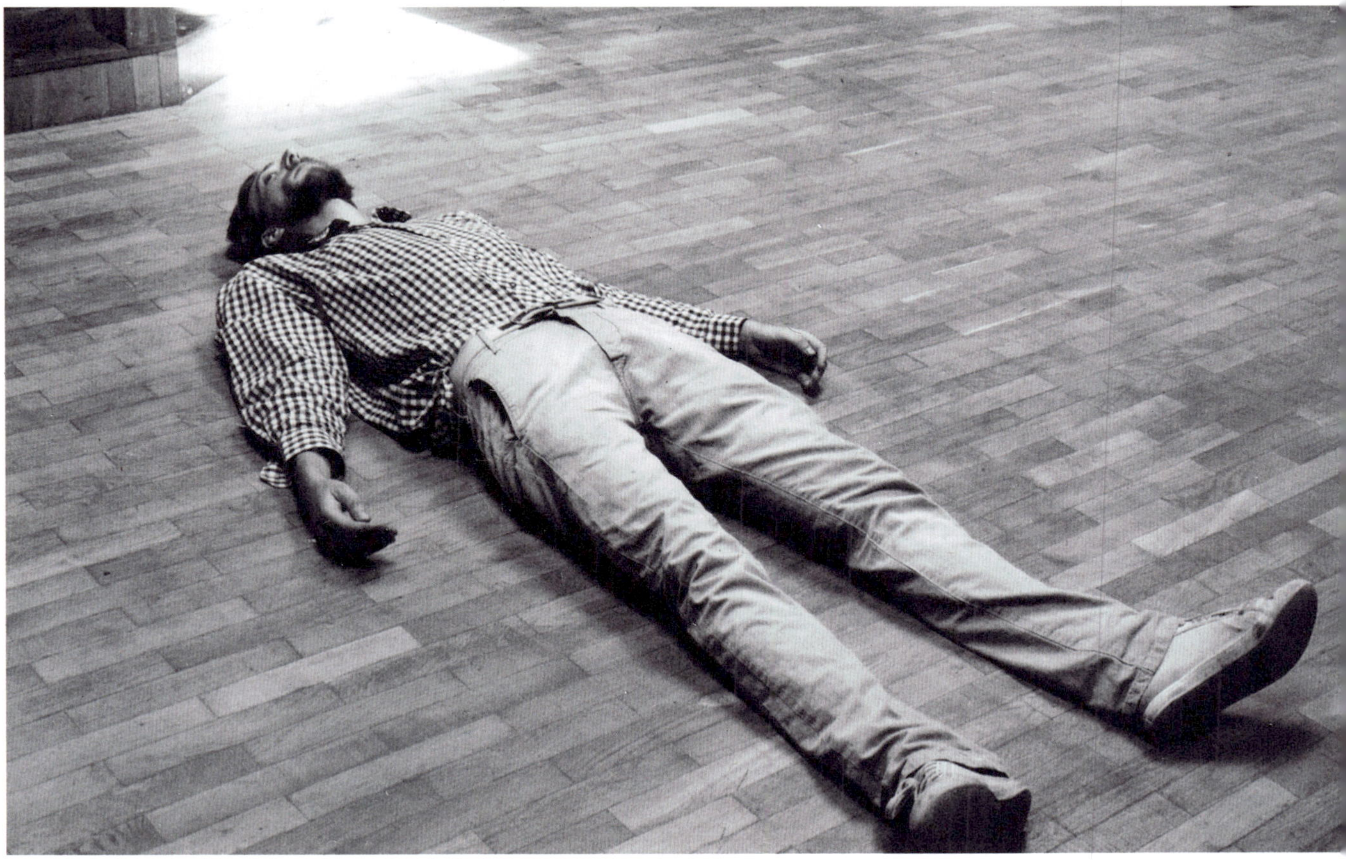

reconstructing the shape of a vanished department store:
KAUFHAUS VRY, during play! Leipzig Festival

→ 156

HERMANN: This is Nuno Lucas and me in 2008, performing *Pongo Land.*

IGOR: What happens in *Pongo Land*?

HERMANN: I would say we pass through a number of physical images, building sculptures together.

IGOR: Building sculptures from two bodies?

HERMANN: Yes, exactly, going from constellation to constellation. Sometimes resembling a strange animal, sometimes a building, working through similarities and differences between our bodies. For me, this collaboration will always have a very special place. We started work without any funding, shortly after finishing *ex.er.ce* in the end of 2007, visiting each other in Lisbon and Leipzig. It's really a work based on friendship, comedy, odd behavior—the beauty that a collaboration can have, in that sense that we were balancing each other. Nuno has much more conceptual rigour than me, which was helping the work a lot.

HERMANN: And this is a few years later, in 2012, a work indirectly linked to *Pongo Land.* A quartet in collaboration with Nuno Lucas, Pieter Ampe and Gui Garrido. Around 2008, more or less at the same time when Nuno and I developed *Pongo Land,* Pieter and Gui had made *Still difficult duet* together. Around 2010, we had the idea to join forces and to collaborate as a quartet, which then premiered in May 2012 at *Kunstenfestivaldesarts* in Brussels. I loved the constellation and it brought me certainly to places I would not go on my own. At the same time, making a performance being of four different minds was a challenging process. Robert Steijn was our dramaturge and partly also therapist.

IGOR: What was the name of that work?

HERMANN: *a coming community.*

IGOR: No less. Agamben.

HERMANN: Yes, which was my idea. Maybe a bit pretentious—

→ 176

IGOR: I don't think it's pretentious. It's what matters to you. To relate collaboration to a concern with the notion of community—which is more spiritual in nature. It's also about nurturing togetherness with people, instead of nurturing your own career. Which is really a good Christian virtue!

HERMANN: Uiuiui!

IGOR: Ha ha ... I don't want to make a big statement out of it. You know that Augustine says, that the source of all evil is arrogance?

HERMANN: Uh.

IGOR: Arrogance as creating preoccupation with yourself, which is creating an addiction. I mean, I'm now interpreting, but if you look through the construction of how Augustine writes about these things it also makes sense. The reason they like him in psychoanalysis is because, in a very different language, he's saying something that psychoanalysis is saying as well: that our sickness stems from the ego, because the ego cannot negotiate relations between different components of reality in any other way but through a form of neurosis. So it generates neurosis as a kind of solution, and by doing that, it's actually setting the stage for some form of unfree life.

HERMANN: Hmm.

IGOR: So there is something about resisting the temptation of self-centeredness. In my opinion, that is very much the core of spirituality. Not only Christianity, but also in Buddhism, it's in everything, everywhere. Where there is a spirit, you need to displace yourself from being in a centre, you know, because the spirit needs space in order to function.

HERMANN: Hmm.

IGOR: It's an ongoing struggle anyway. On one hand, you have a system that requires you to fetishize yourself, because that's how the market operates. And on the other hand, there is a certain resistance to this, which then makes success difficult.

posing in my fathers atelier
for "Performance"

# 20

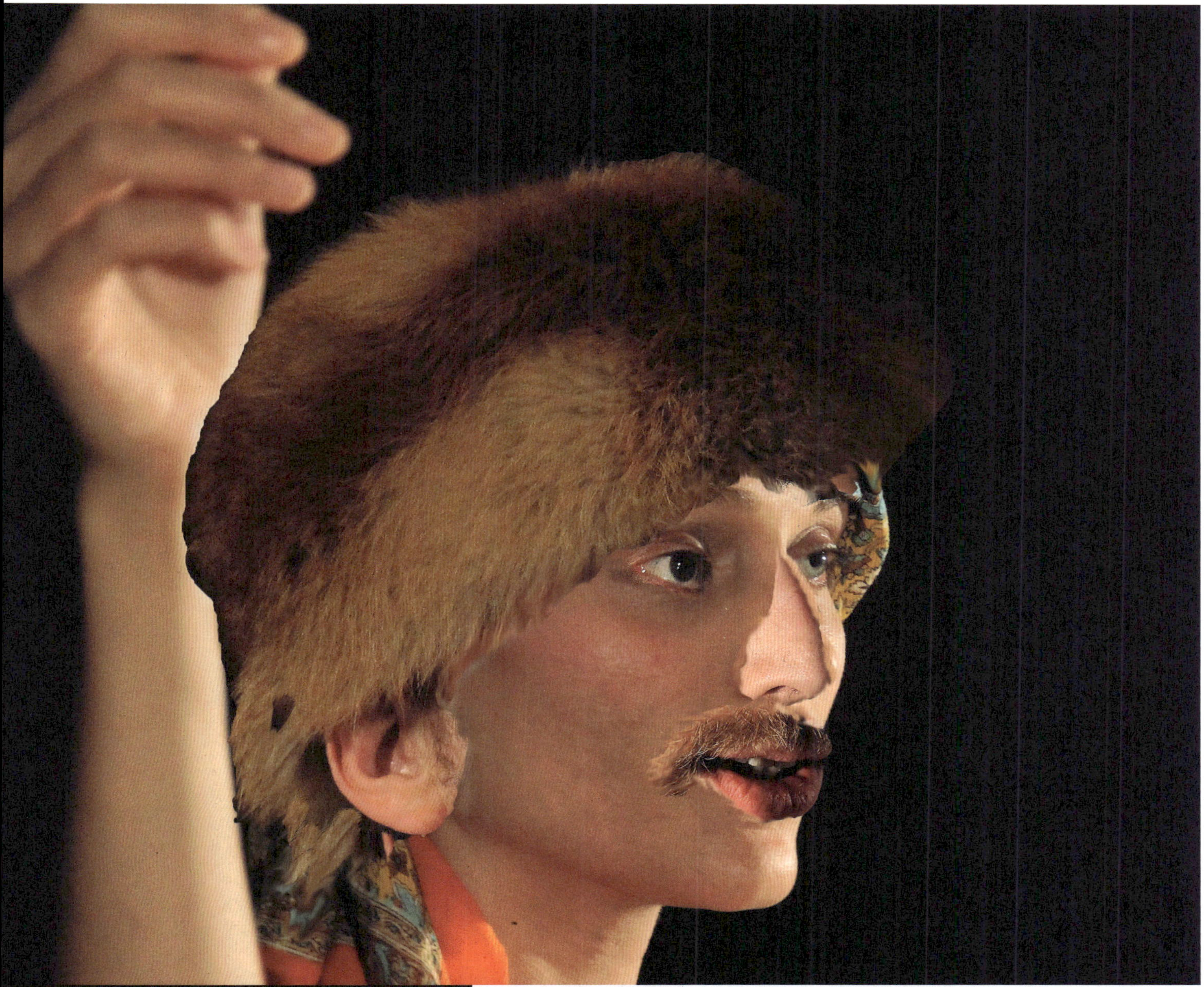

In 2010/2011, Elpida and I started to collaborate, creating a duet called *united states*. This picture is "Hermida", a fusion of our two faces, that we created as an image for the piece, as we were working with the idea of hybridity. → 182

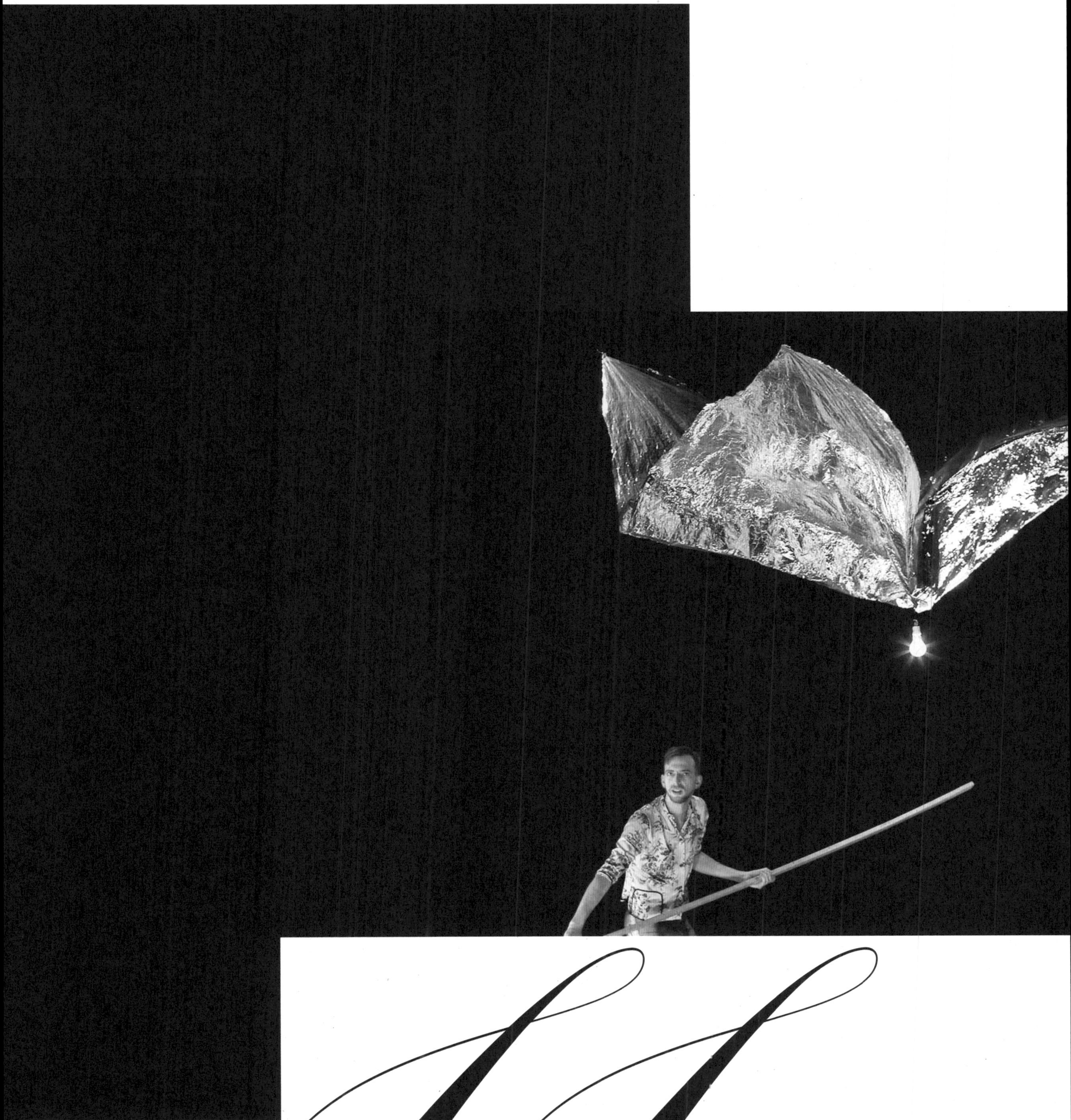

# 2012

→ 156

HERMANN: At different moments, be it in 2002 or 2016, the classic question would come up: „But am I able to make a living out of this?“

IGOR: It's always an open question. But do you consider your work as something which puts you in trouble when it comes to money? Because you have a family and everything—

HERMANN: It's a good question. In some twenty years of freelance work I have become used to a certain underlying stress, having to create a sense of stability while constantly dealing with instability. There is a lot of anti-cyclical thinking involved, on an emotional level it's a challenge to sustain this. But there is also an issue about privilege. For example, there is a property I inherit, the former office of the lottery, which is giving me some security. Sometimes I think, okay, I can or even should take different risks.

IGOR: Yeah, yeah, yeah.

HERMANN: So there is privilege involved, and I am very busy with how to deal with it. Another thing, a side track—I just said that I had to move out of the Berlin apartments I was living in three times, because of renovation work. And each time, there was a little bit of money coming as compensation.

IGOR: Aha?

HERMANN: Like, for example, this car in the picture here, I bought in 2006, from the money that was paid to me for leaving the apartment in Lychener Straße. Or take the apartment in Schönhauser Allee, where I was living together with many dear friends and colleagues: there we got quite some money for moving out. I actually put this money in shares on the stock market.

→ 141

IGOR: The stock market?

HERMANN: Yes. And I was lucky in the years after 2015. It was quite some help for moments where the money coming in from artistic activity would not have been enough.

IGOR: But what do you mean—you invested in shares?

HERMANN: Yes, exactly.

IGOR: Which is a bit of a lottery situation, again.

HERMANN: There is a difference between the lottery and speculation, but both involve a certain relation to the unknown. I tried to say, okay, I only buy stocks of enterprises dealing with renewable energies and based in eastern Germany. And then, out of this principle, I found some interesting stock. Sometimes, I also lost, of course, but in total speculating on the stock market helped me quite a lot in situations I couldn't travel and work as much as before, because of being in a family situation. So in the end, the last years I was able somehow to sustain myself with a lot of luck. It's a juggling process, but also thanks to privilege I was able to do the juggling.

IGOR: Do you feel guilty that you have a privilege? Is there a guilt in you, as a good Catholic?

HERMANN: Of course, yes. But then, in the end it doesn't lead anywhere, to only feel guilty about it. There is this question: a privilege to what? What can you actively do with it, for yourself, but potentially also for other people? Not to hide it, because there's a lot of hidden privilege, specifically in the art scene. There is this high moral attitude connected to art and what it should do, but then, quite often, when there is inheritance involved for example, mysteriously there is no talk about it.

IGOR: That's the time we are living in right now. Where the discourse on privilege is being manipulated in many different ways, and for different purposes.

HERMANN: Yes.

IGOR: And the guilt is also being misused in order to do things that are not always ethical, but that's another subject. Maybe we should go back to follow the images.

"a coming community", developed in collaboration with Nuno Lucas, Gui Garrido & Pieter Ampe

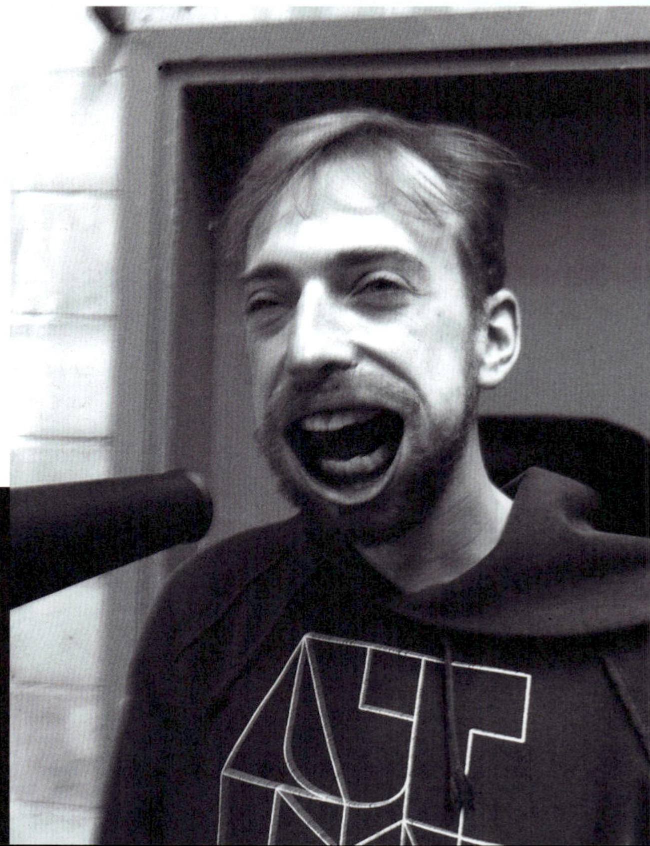

"Bitte" by Thomas Lehmen, Zodiak Helsinki

# 2012

*Slap/Stick*, a solo I created in 2013, when I became a father for the first time. → 105

20

# 13

an inspiration from early on: Wolfgang Krause Zwieback

# 2013

→ 169

IGOR: And when was the first time you worked with Elpida Orfanidou?

HERMANN: We met during *ex.er.ce* in Montpellier in 2007, and two years later I was asking her to join the quartet for *Spielart* Munich, *Themselves already hop!*. And after this, in 2010/2011, Elpida and I started to collaborate, creating a duet called *united states*. This picture is "Hermida", a fusion of our two faces, that we created as an image for the piece, as we were working with the idea of hybridity.

IGOR: This image really inspires that question in me: how do you see your gender?

HERMANN: Hmm.

IGOR: Talking about father. Mother. Man. Woman.

HERMANN: It's not exactly an easy topic for me.

IGOR: Yeah.

HERMANN: I think that I am struggling a lot with gender roles, working as an artist in an environment that includes many different sexualities. And I also love situations where I do not need to define my sexuality completely as one thing or another.

IGOR: Yeah. Yeah.

HERMANN: It's a funny situation; as somebody being in a love relationship with a woman and being a father and all this, I cannot say I do queer art. I would not want to be one of these artists, you know, who claim their work as queer, just because it became fashionable in the field of performing arts.

IGOR: Do you have a desire to claim your work as queer?

HERMANN: For me, there has been an engagement with queerness since the very beginning.

IGOR: That's super important to know. I mean, it's kind of obvious. Because you are making a queer work in terms of what queer means, if we move away a little from the context of identity politics. Because queerness also means to queer a thing or two.

HERMANN: I mean, it's related to lanky bodies as well.

IGOR: Totally. And you have this queerness about you. And it doesn't need to fall into the category of identity politics necessarily.

HERMANN: For example, there are movies that were quite influential for me—for example, I adore Die Bettwurst that Rosa von Praunheim made in 1971; I watched it as a teenager. To me, these pioneers of underground culture are super interesting—their love for people of everyday life, outsiders to the situation they live in... queering a space through a way of talking, a way of dressing, a way of inhabiting. And there's also an interesting balance between artistic choice and non-choice because there's also this love for unintended comedy. This interests me a lot, but as I said, I struggle with claiming queerness in the current field of performing arts.

IGOR: You cannot claim it.

HERMANN: No, I cannot.

IGOR: Well, it's not a question of identity in your case. It's a question of a broader consideration that is now being sanctioned through identity politics, which means that it's becoming unavailable to use. Which opens the question: what to do?

HERMANN: I mean, in the end, I quite trust that this component simply resonates within my work and that the audience will grasp it intuitively. At the same time, it's also really interesting to have been one of the hosts of Fortuna since 2021, which, in addition to being used as a rehearsal and event space, is also a kind of queer living room. And the interim use, which we practice in Fortuna - using a place for a purpose other than the one for which it was originally intended- it has this long story after the fall of communism, but there is as well an essential queer aspect.

# 20

watching a rainbow
while living in Aarhus 2014-2016

Collaborating with Anne Zacho Søgaard and Marina Quesada for "Wir/Nosotros/Vi" in Berlin, Copenhagen & Buenos Aires

"STRTCH", developed and performed with
Tian Rotteveel, May Zarhy & Elpida Orfanidou
Sophiensaele Berlin

# 2014

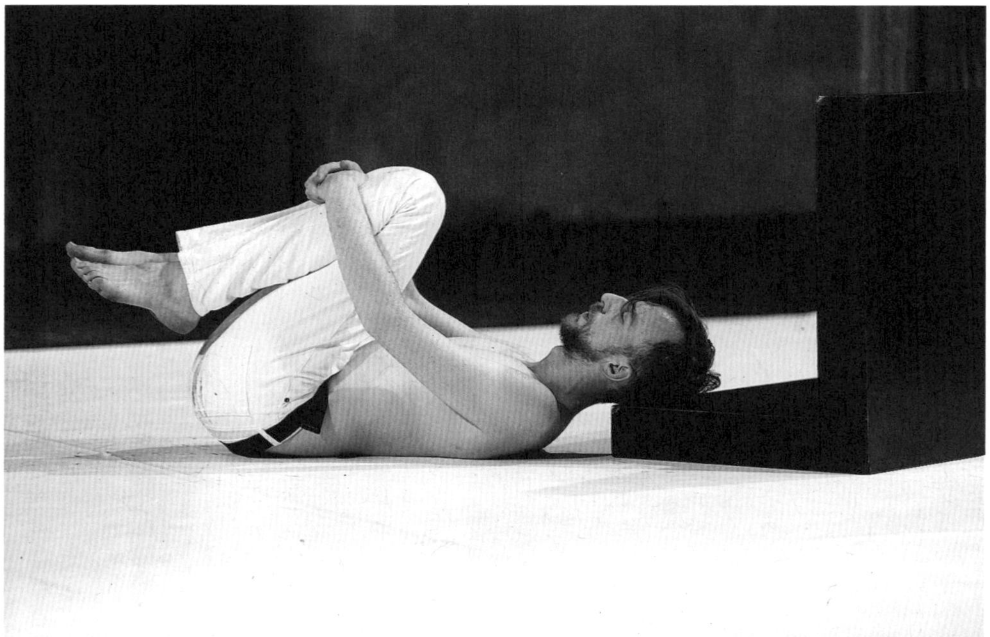

performing in "Former Formen" by July Weber

# 2015

Choreography for "På rejse i min krop", upon Annes invitation, Aarhus Teater

Qui a égaré ma gazelle? with Ali Chahrour and Michaël Phelippeau, Institut Français du Liban, Beirut

→ 202

→ 161

HERMANN: This is *Die Bude*, during its second run in 2017 at Residenz Schauspiel Leipzig. *Die Bude* was an installation and durational performance, a situation somewhere between an animated living room and an exhibition of curiosities. I was moderating the space, creating relationships between guests, objects, plants and some odd drinks. Strangely, the first time I created this work was in 2008, for sommer.bar in *Tanz im August*, only a few months before my mother's parents died. And in 2009, bit by bit, my mother and I would empty out their house in Leipzig, which was filled with objects. And so this question of objects, of inheriting bourgeois traces, and how to deal with them, it has been a topic for me for a long time. To make these objects travel, open them for a different purpose, creating spaces of resonance.

IGOR: And what is this image?

HERMANN: This is our shared apartment in Schönhauser Allee 44.

IGOR: In which year?

HERMANN: I lived there from 2006 to 2011, and later I stayed in the contract until 2015 to be able to still keep the low rent, as I was the main tenant, together with my dear friend and colleague Thomas Proksch. The apartment was located in one of the last few unrenovated buildings in Prenzlauer Berg. A very nice flat, 140 square meters for 626 Euros a month, but heated with coal stoves. It was cold in the winter but fantastic in the summer because of its high ceilings. We hosted so many parties! And a lot of people from the performing arts field passed through this place, living there for a number of weeks or sometimes for years. When we finally had to move out in 2015, we hosted several days of gatherings, parties and performances within the apartment. Here you see *FightClub*, an improvisation score by July Weber for about 15 performers, an alternation of short duets of about one minute, happening in the room I used to live in.

IGOR: There is a certain affinity or exchangeability between private and public.

HERMANN: Yes.

IGOR: Like a permeability between a domain that supposedly is a private one and a domain that is public in a way.

HERMANN: Totally. I am curious about this intersection, and also about the role a host plays within it. How to navigate when the private becomes public or the public becomes private. Making space, but granting space as well. And I think we were instinctively practicing some of this. Today, Fortuna feels partly like a kind of energetic echo of our apartment. Some of the people who run Fortuna as a group, these days Jule Flierl and Thomas Proksch, for example, have been our roommates in Schönhauser Allee 44.

IGOR: There was a community.

HERMANN: Yes, a sense of trust from that time that we lived together. And it is great that this translates into a new group of people, a new context about ten years later.

→ 183

# 2015

Schönhauser Allee 44, after renovation

My role in that context was a little bit the weirdo from the independent scene. → 198

20

collaborating with May Zarhy for "Next to Near", Kelim Choreography Center, Bat Yam, Israël

# 16

"it's in the small things" Pieter Ampe, KVS Brussels

# 2016

HERMANN: And this is 2016 with my dear friend and colleague Tian Rotteveel at Schloss Bellevue together with Joachim Gauck, the German president at the time. And beside Tian is Daniela Schadt, who was the German First lady at that moment.

IGOR: So proper.

HERMANN: Yes!

IGOR: But why were you with them?

HERMANN: It was an evening called "Deutschland tanzt", organized by the German Dance Association to mark a "Year of Dance" in 2016.

IGOR: What were you doing there?

HERMANN: I performed a ten-minute excerpt of *Slap/Stick,* the solo work I had created in 2013.

What I wear is actually the costume from that performance. Tian was with me as he had composed and performed the music—which he did in a fantastic way for a good few of my works. Throughout the evening, there were different ensembles kind of representing dance in Germany. There was Lutz Förster, the long-time Pina Bausch dancer, performing his famous solo from *Nelken.* And I remember a ballet company, I think Bayerisches Staatsballett, and an excerpt from *Aerobics* of Paula Rosolen as well. And I guess my role in that context was a little bit the weirdo from the independent scene. In terms of representation, it was hilarious.

→ 194

IGOR: Fantastic.

HERMANN: Before the evening would begin, all these different dance companies had to stand separately in a salon. And then the presidential couple would come to each company for a picture, with Herr Gauck and Frau Schadt always posing right and left to the company. I really love Tian's pullover in the picture.

IGOR: Yes, very good!

HERMANN: But looking at the picture now, I also think about what you mentioned: the bourgeoisie, the conditioning. Because, looking at my face, there is something—

IGOR: You are in the presence of a president— without any doubt.

HERMANN: There is a nervousness. And for me, this touches on questions about how to deal with political power and its representation, and the ambiguous role artists play in this.
Nevertheless, it was also interesting to perform a solo like *Slap/Stick* in this context, a piece that deals with humor and its anarchic potential. To deal with a space where everything is put orderly in place, to perform seriosity and dignity. I had a lot of joy touching the chandeliers on the wall, playing with their banality, while looking at the faces of the audience. And although it's two different political systems and very different circumstances, it also made me think about the relationships between art and power that my father and grandfather were navigating within GDR cultural politics. Next to the Bellevue picture, I put a photo which I guess was taken at the opening of the X. Kunstausstellung der DDR in Dresden in 1987, where Erich Honecker was shown around the exhibition together with Willi Stoph, Chairman of the Council of Ministers. And there you see another Willi—Willi Sitte, a painter, colleague of my grandfather's and head of the Association of Visual Arts. And at the edge of the picture is my father. Again, I can recognize the similarity of our bodies, the lanky body, the uncomfortability of this situation just a few years before the collapse of the GDR.

→ 194

# 2012

*Die Bude* was an installation and durational performance, a situation somewhere between an animated living room and an exhibition of curiosities. → 190

performing in 'UNDATED", by Martine Pisani

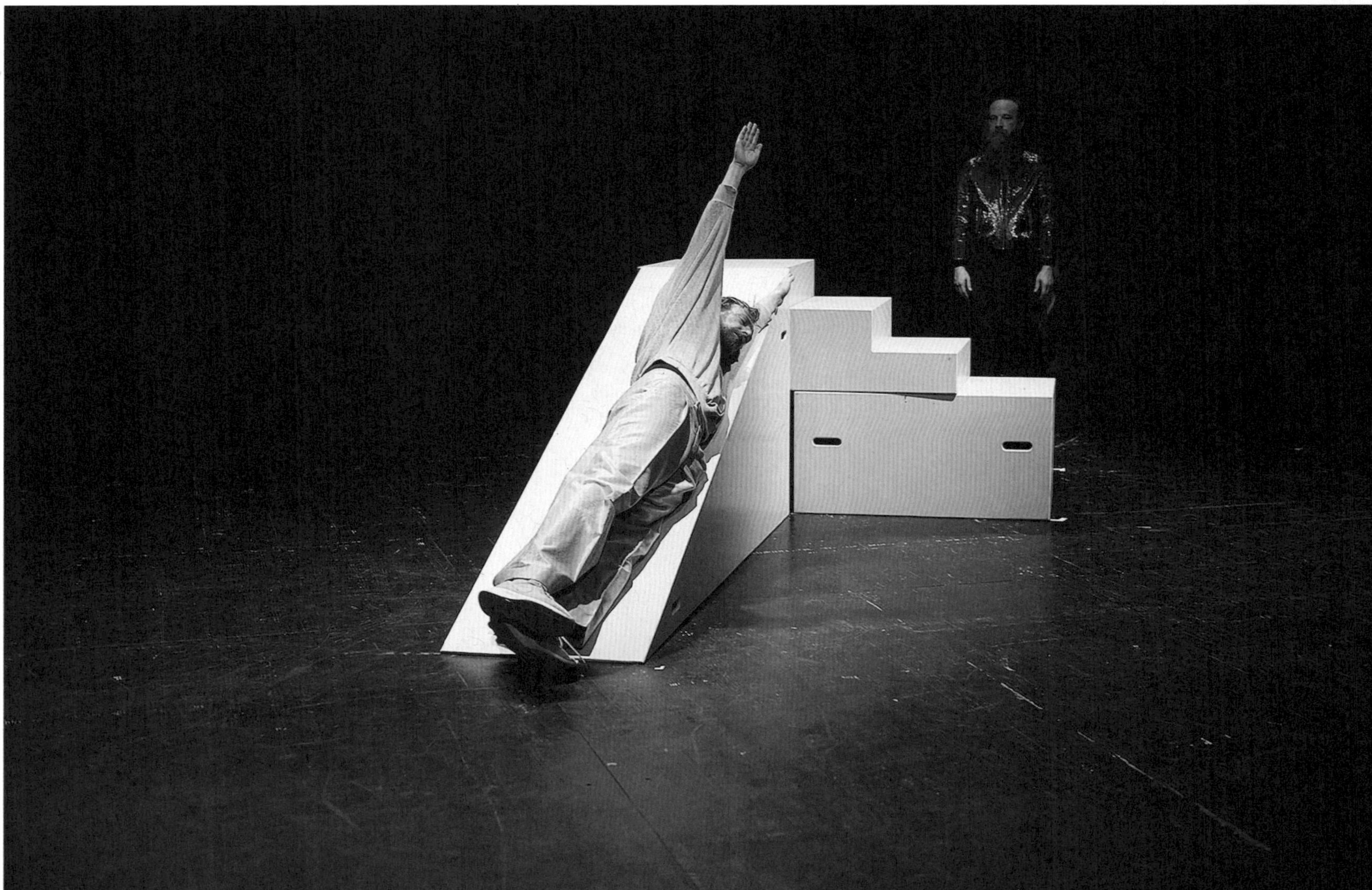

"Slave to the rhythm"
Residenz Schauspiel Leipzig

# 2018

Time passing. Things are sometimes unfolding in strange directions

20

# 18

IGOR: Ultimately, in all of this, you end up making a sequence of performances. Because as in any career of somebody in contemporary dance, at the end of the day, you are creating an oeuvre by moving from one performance to another.

HERMANN: Yes.

IGOR: And there is a collection of performances. So, do you identify your work with this collection, or do you think it is something bigger than that?

HERMANN: Now, while putting these pictures together, I enjoy looking at the bigger picture. Constellations and dynamics that keep coming back, traces, indirect links. At the same time, I'm also not this type of artist who says, okay, this is stage work number one, and then it all builds up on each other.

IGOR: In what sense?

HERMANN: Thinking about artists saying "my work, it just starts at this specific point X, and everything I was doing before is not a part of it". I refuse to be that systematic.

IGOR: The issue of strategy. Many people who are building their careers successfully, in terms of growing into recognition and visibility, are treating the work in the same way, by necessity, which means I make this and then I make this.

HERMANN: Designing a memory.

IGOR: Would you say that you have a different strategy? Or is this just a chance operation? What is the relation between strategy and chance? I don't necessarily need an answer. I am interested in accidents in the history of contemporary art. There is a certain period of time, somewhere between the 1950s and 1970s, when several artists did serious experiments with chance operations. But I always find it fascinating how limited this experimentation was, in relation to the fact that actually, chance is at the core of artistic practice. In general, the tendency in the history of art is to hide it, never really to experiment with it, because it kind of clashes with the notion of the artist-as-genius, whose amazing capacity to make the best choices is certainly not giving the space for something accidental to happen.

HERMANN: Yeah, yeah.

IGOR: I'm saying this because there is an issue here of how we value the role of accidents in artistic production and also in life. Within biography, there is also an issue about the accident, first of all, because that's what every biography essentially is: a collection of accidents and incidents.

HERMANN: Yes.

IGOR: If it is approached honestly, chance has to do with spirit, with spirituality, with the fact that there is something that is not in your hands.

HERMANN: It's funny. I was about to say this before, when we were talking about religion. It's something that I often return to, this feeling of, well, I am not alone and it doesn't depend all on me.

IGOR: Exactly. And that's a very particular perception of reality, and of our place in it. Which is somehow, in my opinion, connected to chance, to opening a space of trust to something other than your own skill. And for me, to trust this "something else" is connected to spirit and inspiration.

HERMANN: Hm.

IGOR: It's a question of you being a vessel for something, like a wind just passing through you. And it's actually this moment of passage, which is the most exciting in the work. So your job is not to treat your work as a thing that you made, but as a process of creating conditions for the spirit to work as well.

HERMANN: Oh, that's very nice.

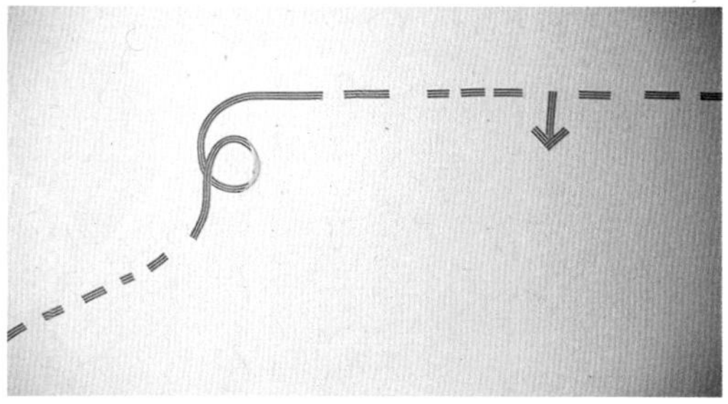
→ 208

# 2019

"singing machine", Sophiensaele Berlin

# 20

"Rhythm is infinite (like the universe, isn't it)" Tanzkongress Hellerau

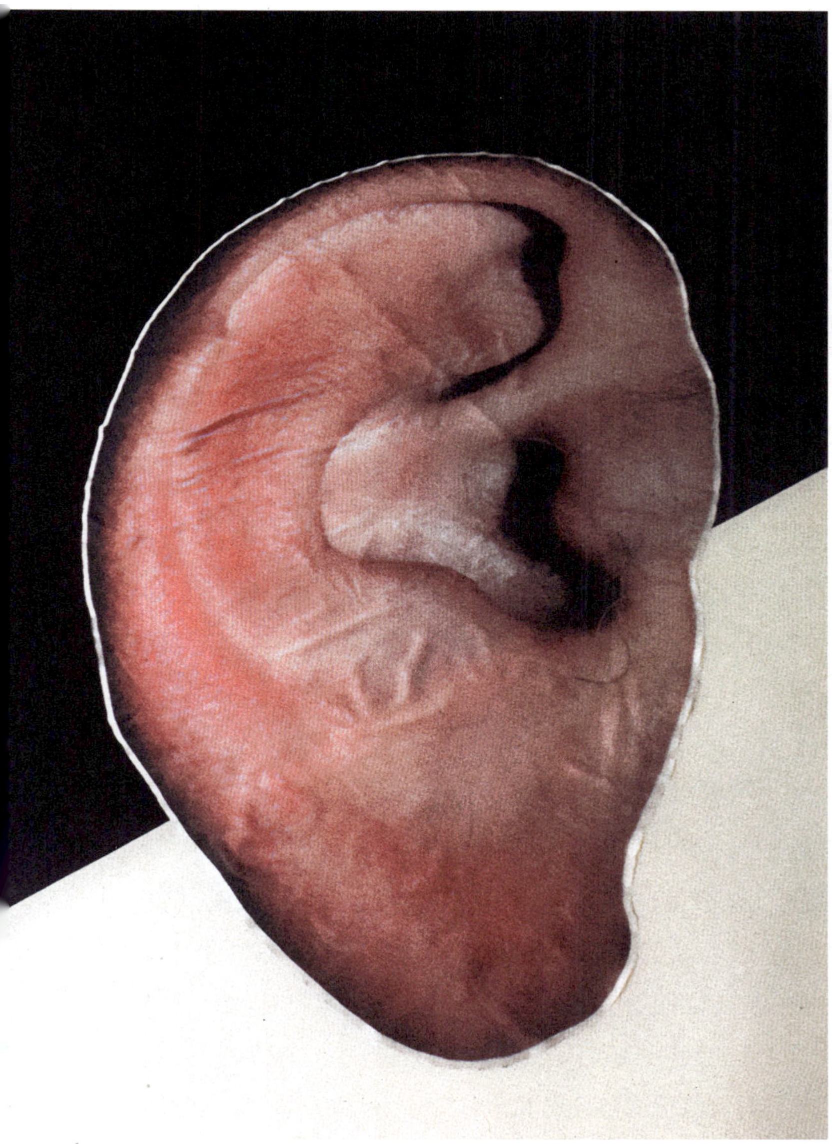

# 19

Time is flying! And we haven't gone through everything.

IGOR: We didn't look at these pictures yet.

HERMANN: Yes. These are pictures of the garden in Pomßen, a place that is on my mind a lot. It's connected to my mother's family, as it's originally the summer house of my great-grandparents. I put it a bit beside the other things, as it is a continuity within this timeline ... A place I've spent a lot of time in various moments of my life so far, I come back every year.

IGOR: It's beautiful.

HERMANN: It's a special place to me— located on the outskirts of Pomßen, a village 25 km southeast of Leipzig. When I was a child, my mother's parents used to spend their summers there, another cosmos of its own within GDR and post-GDR reality, with a particular rhythm and topography.

IGOR: But what is happening there now?

HERMANN: After the death of my grandparents, the garden was inherited by my mother and my cousins Maria Straube and Anna Zett. And only recently, after my mother passed away, it's again a new situation. Together with my cousins and also with our loved ones, we are in conversation about this place and different needs and visions for its future, for example, if it can possibly open up more to the outside world.

IGOR: To open it up in what sense?

HERMANN: Over the last fifteen years, there has already been a dynamic to not treat it as a place that is only related to family, which was more the concept of my grandparents, but to invite other types of relations as well. My mother really looked after the garden in her last years; she already involved her friends more than before, so there are people who over the years regularly come and developed a relation to the place. At the same time, within the last years, my cousin Anna Zett started to be engaged in a new way, through hosting her friends and artist colleagues, and as well through a lot of building and renovation work.

IGOR: This is a huge garden.

HERMANN: Originally, it used to be a farm. My mother's grandfather, the one that opened the lottery, bought it in 1927 and turned it into a kind of park. It's a constant commitment to maintain it, every now and then, trees die or fall off, specifically now with climate change, and the years of drought after 2018. And who knows if the garden would exist today without the help of Wolfgang Mietz, a craftsman living in the village, employed by my grandfather for more than 40 years, and a friend of my childhood and youth with an enormous talent to repair and improvise. When I am in Pomßen, my mind is busy differently—I rarely would rehearse there, like in a city; I would rather paint a bench or cut a little tree, for example. But at the same time, of course, art does play a role. For example, within the collaboration with Anna Zett we are in a double role, both being artists with some shared interests and family members sharing a garden connected to a complex story of family relations. So there is a field of dialogue, conflict, and collaboration on many levels, but I have a lot of trust in art and its transformative powers. Maybe there is a way to maintain the garden in Pomßen as a space with a specific timing and history, but in a way that invites change. Also, the garden is located in an area where the challenges in rural Eastern Germany are quite visible, including the rise of right-wing populism, and the question of what to do about it becomes quite concrete here. Many things from my childhood have vanished, but, weirdly enough, this spot remains. But it's also a garden, not an object. It is by nature in constant transformation, growth, and decay happening at the same time. And actually, over many years, it has gradually become more and more wild.

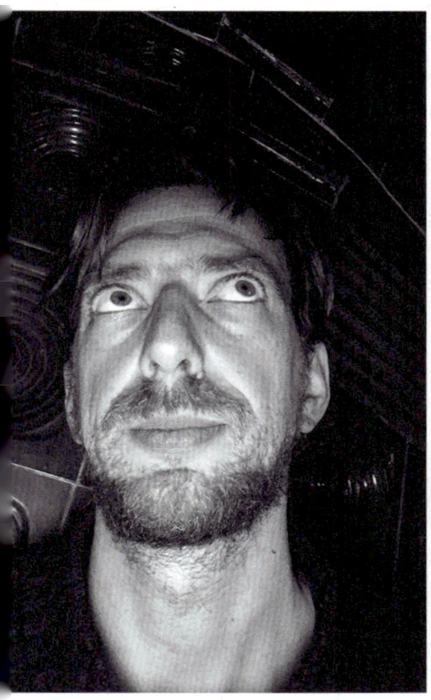

# 2020

„Ausblick", Johannes Heisig

# 20

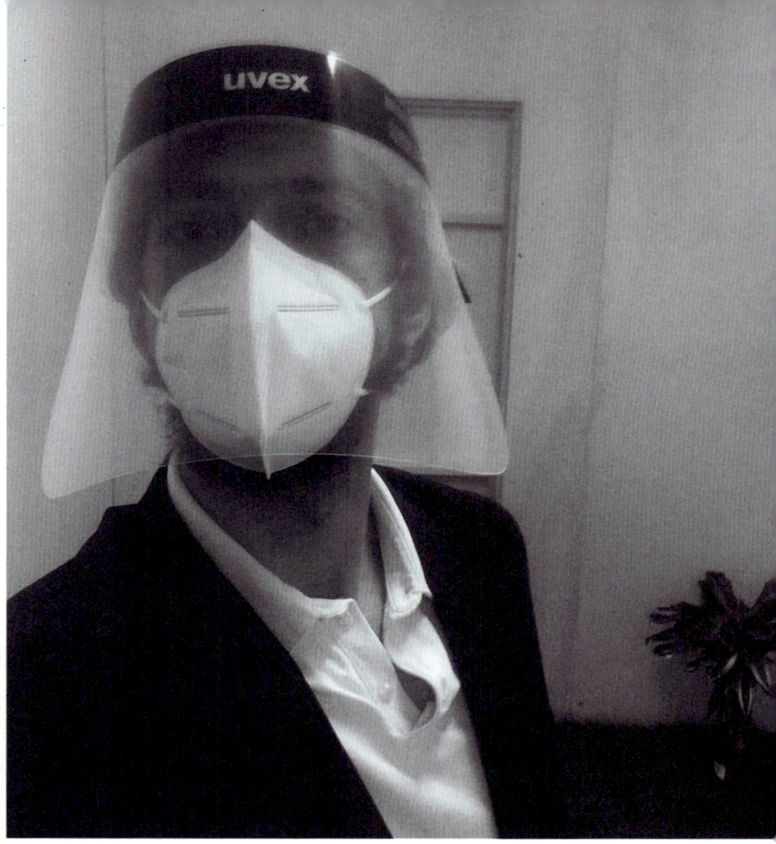

# 20

"Resonanz - post socialist group improvisation"
participatory research with Anna Zett

collaborating with Angelika Waniek
for "Ich steh auf und setz mich wieder hin
(Feste des Handelns) Leipzig, Schaubühne

with Gabriele Stötzer, Angelika Waniek, Anna Zett

# 2021

IGOR: But how does Fortuna work? What is the practice of it?

HERMANN: Fortuna Wetten was originally a betting office at Karl-Marx-Strasse 127 in Neukölln. For a longer time, I had the fantasy of working in an empty shop, and thanks to Tanzpakt Reconnect, a project financed by the government's COVID-19 emergency fund Neustart Kultur—which ultimately also finances this book (danke!)—I could rent the space for three weeks in October 2021. During this phase, I invited different colleagues for a shared research, and out of this, the nucleus of a group emerged.

IGOR: And is the financial base in terms of the continued existence of this space provided through you?

HERMANN: Not anymore. In the very beginning, at the end of 2021, I continued paying the rent for additional weeks to keep the place, and new people joined. Slowly, we built a structure where people would find out who can contribute what, and **Fortuna emerged as a self-organized space at the interface of choreographic research and community work.** It's now run by a group of about ten people, some of them individual artists, others organized in collectives, hosting activities from dance classes to meditation, social gatherings to body work or smaller concerts. In the beginning, it was mostly Neustart Kultur money that we pooled, in order to share the monthly rent for the space.

IGOR: From your individual support grants?

HERMANN: Yes. Because in these weird times of the pandemic, suddenly there was more state funding available which was not tied to the creation of stage works.

IGOR: Suddenly it was possible to do these things.
HERMANN: Yes, but at the same time, these support grants were distributed very unevenly. So Fortuna was also connected to the idea of pooling these by creating space where people are not required to contribute an equal amount, but everyone contributes according to the possibilities of the moment.
IGOR: That's pure Marxism! How does it go? The famous sentence, which we in Yugoslavia repeated endlessly—uh huh—everybody according to—There is a famous sentence!
HERMANN: I can imagine that there is a proper sentence.
IGOR: Ah! Karl Marx said: From each according to his ability, to each according to his needs. Kind of the core of communist ideology in terms of practical economy. This famous sentence that is both a promise and the failure of communism. Because in Yugoslavia, ultimately, there was a certain cynicism about the notion of social ownership.
HERMANN: Of social ownership?
IGOR: Yeah, goods not privately owned by anybody but belonging to everybody. Which, ultimately, cynically, was always considered to mean that nobody cares.
HERMANN: That's always the danger, in many shared spaces, also here in Fortuna. With many things, no one knows exactly where they come from or what their original intention was. But even if I sometimes get overwhelmed, there is a part in me that quite likes this.
IGOR: Maybe there is something about Nobody Cares which also connects to anarchism and to a certain chaos which can be perceived as a problem, but in the end, it is also a potential, an opportunity.
HERMANN: Possible, possible!

Fortuna emerged as a self-organized space at the interface of choreographic research and community work. → 222

# 2021

# 2022

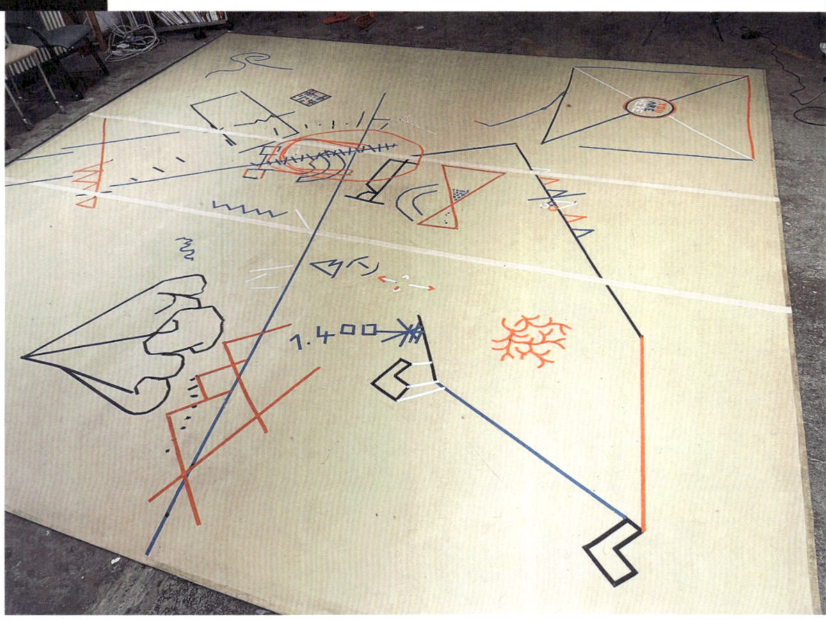

We created a participatory format for smaller and larger groups of people, where personal associations with the GDR and what came after are being activated and responded to. → 228

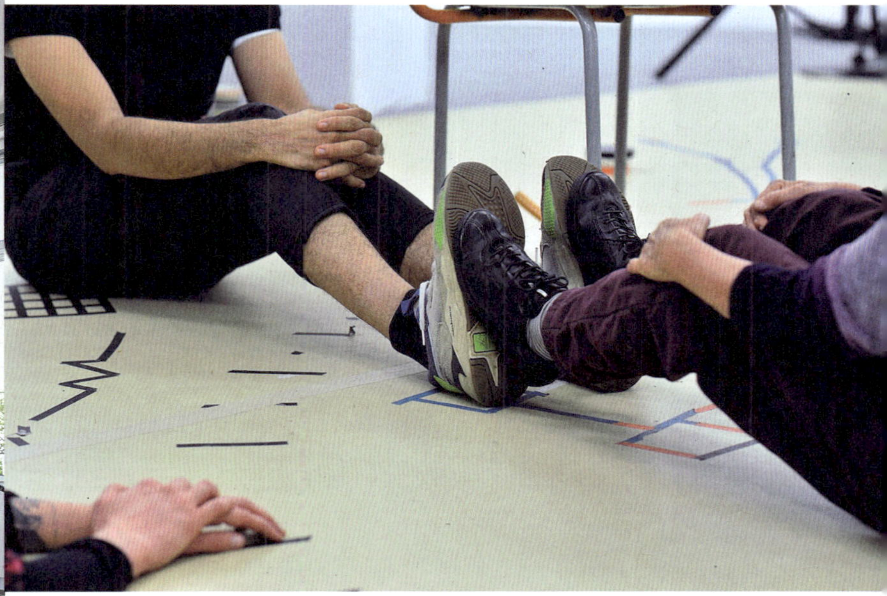

HERMANN: And there is also this connection to chance, in the sense of putting yourself in a situation where you perceive differently, because you let yourself drift. You don't go the way you go every day. To me, the situationist idea of the "Dérive" is still very interesting today, in the sense of an unplanned journey through a landscape by letting ourselves "be drawn by the attractions of the terrain and the encounters we find there". So there's something about perception, a relation between drifting and chance operation.

IGOR: Yeah, yeah. Because it allows for otherness to take place, also allowing for spirit to pass through.

HERMANN: For sure. It's about a work on the mindset you put yourself into when leaving the door. For what encounters do you prepare yourself? How long do you stay in each spot? When do you choose to cross to the other side of the street? Or how do you deal with time?

IGOR: And I think queerness also falls into this category. It's about drifting away from who you are, according to the rules—of any kind. Be it the rules of society, of a bourgeois family, or the rules of the church. Or also the rules of an artistic community.

→ 227

HERMANN: Talking about the church and the bourgeoisie: it's an ongoing conversation with my cousin Anna Zett, who works as an artist, filmmaker and writer. With her, I share growing up in this bourgeois and Christian bubble within communism, and we have different ways of dealing with it. I am very happy that out of this experience we could develop an artistic research project called *Resonanz – Postsocialist Group Improvisation*. We created a participatory format for smaller and larger groups of people, where personal associations with the GDR and what came after are being activated and responded to. It feels like a long-term process, and I am still very curious where it will lead. When Anna and I were growing up in the 1980s, we encountered these institutions, the bourgeois family and the church, in a

→ 57

moment of crisis. Marginalised during communism, but still existing in niches.

IGOR: Yeah, yeah.

HERMANN: Very different from the old "West", where these systems of bourgeois family or of the church were unbroken and much more oppressive than in the context we were growing up in. Because of this, I even have the tendency, maybe unlike my cousin Anna, to prevent these institutions from falling apart.

IGOR: Yeah, yeah. But the thing is that every institution, at a certain point of social development, becomes queer. Because the church, in a society which is completely secular, is a queer phenomenon.

HERMANN: It's true.

IGOR: Because when you can observe the priests with enough distance to see how bizarre this whole thing is, it's absolutely queer. And also the rules of a bourgeois family can become queer in a certain context—resisting the movement of their surroundings.

HERMANN: Exactly. Sometimes you resist by being left behind.

IGOR: Yes. You don't always resist from going in front or going to the side. To still exist, that is a form of queerness as well, which is an interesting thought that I never had before.

And then, all of a sudden, you can still access this phenomenon without being dismissive or judgemental about it. That's a funny thought, to reveal both church and family as queer phenomena and embrace them rather than criticise them, in order to transform them rather than reject them, which would make them even more conservative. An interesting operation ...

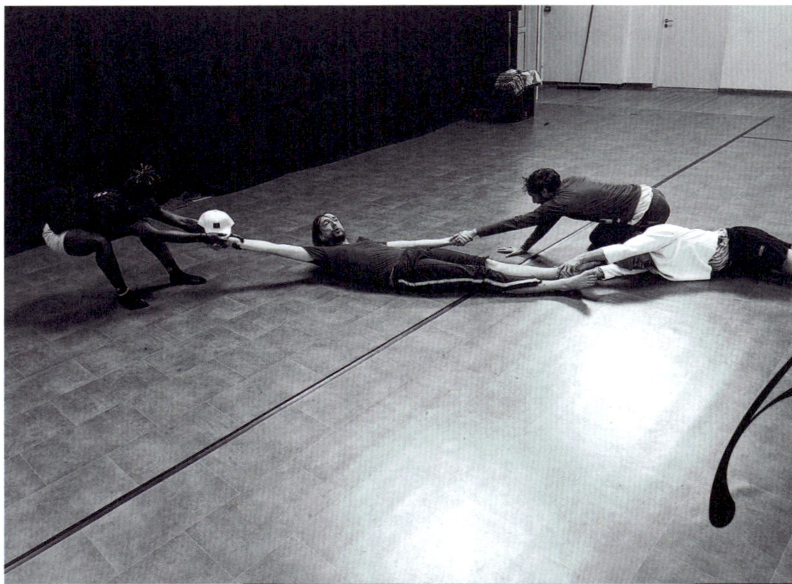

Time is flying! And we are
not completely through everything

## Catalogue of works Hermann Heisig

### Late Night Dada (2024)

IDEA, ARTISTIC DIRECTION: Hermann Heisig
BY AND WITH: Hermann Heisig, Anja Müller, Elpida Orfanidou, Thomas Proksch
STAGE, PERFORMANCE, COSTUMES: Lea Kieffer, Timothée Nay
SPECIAL APPEARANCE: Roger Sala Reyner
COACHING, DRAMATURGY: Igor Dobričić, Joséphine Evrard, Anne Zacho Søgaard
VIDEO, DOCUMENTATION: Sini Pfalzer
ASSISTANCE: Aliès Mané
PRODUCTION MANAGEMENT: Susanne Ogan
DISTRIBUTION: Leonie Kusterer

### FORTUNA (2021–2024)

In cooperation with Social Pleasure Center, Thomas Proksch, Tümay Kılınçel, Jule Flierl, Anne Zacho Søgaard, Olympia Bukkakis, TENT Collective, Backbone Berlin (Barbara Greiner, Sarah Parolin)
CO-FOUNDED BY (GRÜNDUNGSORGANISATION): Leonie Kusterer

### Happy Sisyphos (2022)

IDEA: Hermann Heisig
PERFORMANCE: Hermann Heisig, Ayşe Orhon, Thomas Proksch
MUSIC: Thomas Proksch
DRAMATURGY: Anne Zacho Søgaard
PRODUCTION: fabrik Potsdam as part of explore dance – Network Dance for Young Audiences

### Ich steh auf und setz mich wieder hin (Feste des Handelns) (I stand up and sit down again (Celebrations of Action) (2022)

IDEA, PERFORMANCE: Hermann Heisig, Angelika Waniek
SOUND: Lorenz Lindner
With the participation of the artists Robin Arthur, Zwoisy Mears-Clarke, Gabriele Stötzer, Sonny Thet and the "Flying Forum" from the Plus X collective
PRODUCTION MANAGEMENT: Kristina Patzelt
Co-production with KATAPULT – Performance Plattform Leipzig
In cooperation with the ETTERSBERG FOUNDATION – Memorial and Education Centre Andreasstraße, Erfurt

### keep on – SCHALLGARTEN reconnected (2020–2023)

IDEA: Hermann Heisig
BY AND WITH: Hermann Heisig, Elpida Orfanidou, Thomas Proksch, Roger Sala Reyner
SPATIAL CONCEPT, COSTUMES: Lea Kieffer
DRAMATURGY: Igor Dobričić
PRODUCTION MANAGEMENT: Susanne Ogan
In cooperation with Étape Danse – Bureau du Théâtre et de la Danse / Institut français Germany in collaboration with

fabrik Potsdam, La Maison – Centre de Développement Chorégraphique National – Uzès Gard Occitanie, Théâtre de Nîmes, INTERPLAY Turin / Fondazione Piemonte dal Vivo – PDV (Circuito Regionale Multidisciplinare del Piemonte) – Lavanderia a Vapore

## RESONANZ – Postsocialist Group Improvisation (2020–2022)

BY AND WITH: Hermann Heisig, Anna Zett
SPATIAL DESIGN: wkc
SOUND CONCEPT: Tian Rotteveel
MUSIC: Matti Gajek, Tian Rotteveel
PERFORMATIVE CO-RESEARCH: Jule Flierl, Rike Flämig, Philipp Goll, Lydia Lierke, Maru Mushtrieva, Minh Duc Pham, David Polzin, Anna Stiede, Kristof Trakal, Ute Waldhausen, Monika Zimmering and others
LIGHTING CONSULTANT: Annegret Schalke
TEXT, TECHNOLOGY, PROCESS DOCUMENTATION: Anna Zett
PRODUCTION MANAGEMENT: Susanne Ogan

## Singing Machine (2019)

BY AND WITH: Hermann Heisig
MUSIC: Tian Rotteveel
OBJECTS, COSTUME, STAGE: Julian Weber
DRAMATURGY: Igor Dobričić
LIGHT DESIGN: Benjamin Schälike
PRODUCTION MANAGEMENT: Susanne Ogan
Co-production with SOPHIENSÆLE

## Slave to the rhythm (2018)

IDEA: Hermann Heisig
BY AND WITH: Pieter Ampe, Jessica Batut, Hermann Heisig, Elpida Orfanidou, Alma Toaspern
MUSIC: Gunnar Wendel aka Kassem Mosse
STAGE, COSTUMES: Marie Gerstenberger
LIGHTING DESIGN: Thomas Achtner
PRODUCTION MANAGEMENT: Susanne Ogan
Coproduction with Schauspiel Leipzig and HELLERAU – European Center for the Arts Dresden

## Lindenau Re-Visited (2017)

BY AND WITH: Hermann Heisig, Diana Wesser
VIDEO, SOUND: Sophie Stephan / ZOFIA, Diana Wesser
LIGHTING DESIGN CONSULTANT: Thomas Achtner
OUTSIDE EYES: Katharina Morawe, Patrick Primavesi, Anne Zacho Søgaard, Alma Toaspern
PRODUCTION MANAGER: Susanne Ogan
In cooperation with LOFFT – Das Theater and Leipzig University / Institute for Theater Studies

## NEXT TO NEAR (2016)

IDEA, CHOREOGRAPHY, PERFORMANCE: Hermann Heisig, May Zarhy
COMPOSITION, MUSIC, OUTSIDE EYE: Tian Rotteveel
FLUTE: Rowan Hamwood
BASS: Giuseppe Bottiglieri
LIGHT DESIGN: Sandra Blatterer
LIGHT: Fabian Bleisch
STAGE, COSTUME: Marie Gerstenberger, Lea Søvsø
KUBUS: lost & found Aarhus
CUBE: Amir Weiser
PRODUCTION MANAGEMENT: Susanne Ogan, Johanna Milz (MAMAZA)
Co-production with MAMAZA and SOPHIENSÆLE, Künstlerhaus Mousonturm Frankfurt, Schaubühne Lindenfels Leipzig and Kelim – Choreography Center Bat Yam, Israel

## Qui a egaré ma gazelle? (2015)

CONCEPT, CHOREOGRAPHY: Ali Chahrour, Hermann Heisig, Mickaël Phelippeau
Initiated by Goethe-Institut Beirut and Institut français du Liban

## STRTCH (2014)

IDEA: Hermann Heisig
BY AND WITH: Hermann Heisig, Elpida Orfanidou, Tian Rotteveel
MUSIC: Tian Rotteveel
STAGE, OBJECTS: Jaka Plešec
LIGHTING DESIGN: Benjamin Schälike
OUTSIDE AND INSIDE EYE: May Zarhy
ASSISTANT: Benjamin Coyle
PRODUCTION MANAGEMENT: Susanne Ogan
Co-production with SOPHIENSÆLE and HELLERAU – European Center for the Arts Dresden

## Wir / nosotros / vi (2013)

BY AND WITH: Hermann Heisig, Marina Quesada, Anne Zacho Søgaard
DRAMATURGY: Anna K. Becker
LIGHT DESIGN: Sandra Blatterer
SOUND DESIGN: Axel Krygier
PRODUCTION MANAGEMENT: Susanne Ogan
Co-production with SOPHIENSÆLE

## příští zastávka (2013) / naeste stoppested (2017)

BY AND WITH: Hermann Heisig
Co-production with Brno House of Arts and Aarhus Teater as part of Udflugten (2017)

## SLAP / STICK (2013)

BY AND WITH: Hermann Heisig
MUSIC: Tian Rotteveel
LIGHT DESIGN: Benjamin Schälike
INSTALLATION: Jaka Plešec
OUTSIDE EYES: Nuno Lucas, Elpida Orfanidou, Anna Volkland, Silke Z.
PRODUCTION MANAGEMENT: Susanne Ogan
Coproduction with tanz.tausch and SOPHIENSÆLE

## a coming community (2012)

BY AND WITH: Pieter Ampe, Guilherme Garrido, Hermann Heisig, Nuno Lucas
DRAMATURGY: Louise Van den Eede
OUTSIDE EYE: Robert Steijn
Co-production with CAMPO Ghent, Kunstenfestivaldesarts Brussels, Alkantara Lissabon, Tanz im August / Hebbel am Ufer Berlin, La Bâtie-Festival de Genève and NXTSTP

## united states (2011)

BY AND WITH: Hermann Heisig, Elpida Orfanidou
MUSIC, DRAMATURGY: Gerald Kurdian
LIGHT DESIGN: Sandra Blatterer
INSTALLATION: Jaka Plešec
PRODUCTION MANAGEMENT: Susanne Ogan
Co-production with Student Centre Zagreb & TD Theatre-Culture of Change, Goethe-Institut Zagreb, Hebbel am Ufer, Berlin, TanzWerkstatt Berlin, Schaubühne Lindenfels and fabrik Potsdam as part of the Artist-in-Residence program

## KAUFHAUS URY (2010/2015)

BY AND WITH: Hermann Heisig
Co-production with play! Leipzig Festival and Tanzarchiv Leipzig e. V., B_Tour Festival (2015)

## Themselves already Hop! (2009)

IDEA: Hermann Heisig
BY AND WITH: Nuno Lucas, Elpida Orfanidou, Thomas Proksch, Esther-Maria Quade
MUSIC: Andrew Pekler
LIGHT DESIGN: Sandra Blatterer
COSTUME: Laura Leth Meilvang
DRAMATURGY: Dennis Deter
MENTORING: Meg Stuart
PRODUCTION DRAMATURGY: Susanne Ogan
PRODUCTION MANAGEMENT: Marc Pohl
Co-production with SOPHIENSÆLE, Heisig / Lucas GbR and Spielmotor Munich

## What Comes Up / Must Go Up (2009)

BY AND WITH: Hermann Heisig, Nuno Lucas, Irina Müller
LIGHTING DESIGN: Wassan Ali
COACHING: Miguel Pereira
PRODUCTION MANAGEMENT: Susanne Ogan
Co-production with LOOPING 2009, an initiative of Uzès Danse (France), TanzWerkstatt Berlin (Germany) and O Espaço do Tempo (Portugal), fabrik Potsdam as part of Tanzplan Potsdam: Artist-in-Residence

## DIE BUDE (2008/2017)

BY AND WITH: Hermann Heisig
Cooperation Sommer.bar 08, Podewil Berlin, Residency Schauspiel Leipzig (2017)

## Pongo Land (2008)

BY AND WITH: Nuno Lucas, Hermann Heisig
THANKS TO: Florent Delval, Madeleine Fournier, Christabel Heisig, Johannes Heisig, Maria Lucas, João Lucas, Beby Raza, Theo Solnik, André Theriault, Anne Zacho Søgaard
Co-production with Collective Consciousness and Théâtre de l'Usine Genève with the support of TanzWerkstatt Berlin, CENTA, Forum Dança, ACCCA

## In this beautif. Countryside (2008)

BY AND WITH: Hermann Heisig
MUSIC: Andrew Pekler
STAGE: Robert-Christian Friebe
OUTSIDE EYES: Nuno Lucas, Claire Vivianne Sobottke, Marina Quesada
Co-production with Tanztage Berlin

## RANDSHOW (2006)

IDEA: Hermann Heisig, Anne Zacho Søgaard
BY AND WITH: Hermann Heisig, Ronny Hofmann, Louise Ry Mathiasen, Thomas Proksch, Marina Quesada, Claire Vivianne Sobottke, Diana Wesser, Anne Zacho Søgaard
Co-production with Moderne Nerven (Germany), nachBerlin (Denmark)

## Abhanden kommen / Die Landschaft (2005)

IDEA: Hermann Heisig, Marina Quesada
BY AND WITH: Caroline Decker, Hermann Heisig, Marina Quesada, Vivien Roos, Anne Zacho Søgaard
MUSIC: Andrew Pekler
LIGHT DESIGN: Sandra Blatterer
Co-production with Moderne Nerven and DOCK 11

Hermann Heisig
Timing

by and with Hermann Heisig

DRAMATURGY:
Igor Dobričić
COLLABORATION:
Susanne Ogan, Leonie Kusterer
EDITORIAL TEAM SPECTOR BOOKS:
Christin Krause, Jan Wenzel
PROOFREADING:
Jan Caspers
DESIGN:
Natasha Agapova
LITHOGRAPHY:
Aleksey Novikov

CREDITS:
Diego Agulló, Pieter Ampe, Anat Amrani, ANTOINETTE, Rolf Arnold, Thomas Aurin, Katrine Breidahl, Silke Briel, Bernd Cramer, Laura Deschner, Doris Dziersk, Michael Ehritt, Christiane Eisler, Dieter Hartwig, Christabel Heisig, Johannes Heisig, Reinout Hiel, Lea Kieffer, Barbara Klemm, Anna Kolata, Tamar Lamm, Oliver Look, Nuno Lucas, Ute Novieku, Regina Purschwitz, Margarida Ribeiro, Brunhild Schmidt-Eisler, Maria Schmidt-Lorenz, Michaela Schweiger, Anne Zacho Søgaard, Theo Solnik, Rudolf Straube, Helfried Strauß, Vincent Thomasset, Dorothea Tuch, July Weber, Gabriel Weichert, Diana Wesser, André Wunstorf

Special thanks go to Bureau Ritter / TANZPAKT RECONNECT for financial support, to Christin Krause, Susanne Ogan, Leonie Kusterer, and Natasha Agapova for their guidance during the process, to Anne Zacho Søgaard, Edith Zacho Heisig, and Maja Zacho Heisig for their patience with a metal rooster and to Nancy Böttner, Mor Demer, Sergio Edelsztein, Jule Flierl, Johannes Heisig, Nuno Lucas, Sarah-Judith Mettke, Anja Müller, Elpida Orfanidou, Thomas Proksch, Marcus Psurek, Marina Quesada, Gabriel Weichert, Diana Wesser, May Zarhy, and Anna Zett for eyes, ears, and feedback.

Supported by Bureau Ritter / TANZPAKT RECONNECT, which is funded by the German Federal Government Commissioner for Culture and the Media, as part of the NEUSTART KULTUR initiative.

Die Beauftragte der Bundesregierung für Kultur und Medien

PUBLISHED BY
Spector Books
Harkortstraße 10
04107 Leipzig
www.spectorbooks.com

DISTRIBUTION:
Germany, Austria: GVA, Gemeinsame Verlagsauslieferung Göttingen GmbH&Co. KG, www.gva-verlage.de
Switzerland: AVA Verlagsauslieferung AG, www.ava.ch
France, Belgium: Interart Paris, www.interart.fr
UK: Central Books Ltd, www.centralbooks.com
USA, Canada, Central and South America, Africa: ARTBOOK / D.A.P., www.artbook.com
South Korea: The Book Society, www.thebooksociety.org
Japan: twelvebooks, www.twelve-books.com
Australia, New Zealand: Perimeter Distribution, www.perimeterdistribution.com

© 2025 Spector Books, Leipzig

First edition: 2025

Printed in Germany

English edition
ISBN 978-3-95905-732-5

German edition
ISBN 978-3-95905-731-8